TRANSLATING PAINT

by

Anneke Baeten

D1531245

Post-Asemic Press

Post-Asemic Press 005

ISBN-13: 978-1-7328788-4-6

Contact: postasemicpress@gmail.com

postasemicpress.blogspot.com

Cover art by Anneke Baeten

Foreword

Translating paint is a serious business. Anneke makes one or more broad brushstrokes, which are translucent. Tracks and channels where the hairs of the brush dragged paint across the paper are visible. Then she has to explain them, by translating them into thinner strokes which resemble handwriting, which she calls "asemic writing". If there are gaps or stutters in the broad brushstrokes, the thinner lines of writing surround and complement them.

The brushstrokes are closer to pure image, and spontaneous thoughts. The asemic writing is closer to paragraphs or other textual forms, and slow, reflective thought.

However, translating paint is also fun. Many of the titles, which Anneke tells me she chose either in the middle of a composition or at the end, have a humorous edge to them. Topics implied by the titles include discourse analysis (A Pointless Dialogue), cosmic ideas (A Universal Message), cosmic jokes (Dwarf planet annoyed at pigeonhole-ing) and jokes about what is on the page (sneaky-interfering-snake-again).

Asemic writing is a thriving international phenomenon, with a history extending back centuries – as far back as Tang Dynasty calligrapher "Crazy" Zhang Xu. Attempting to uncover what wordless writing or illegible writing means is possibly its most difficult aspect.

Anneke goes through 3 stages of creation and translation, making a shape with a brush, attempting to write about (and around) that shape without using words, and assigning a title in English words to the composition. Actually, there's a fourth stage, photographing each page. The originals are on A3 paper, considerably larger than the page you are reading now. Anneke's photographs of her handiwork compress the size and in some cases peer obliquely rather than from directly above. The oblique views give me the impression that I'm looking at something larger. A fifth stage or series of stages is that the photographs were compiled into a book, printed on paper and delivered to a reader.

The asemic writing must have been done in a meditative state of mind. Its rhythms are harmonious. I'm reminded of the patterns insects describe when they are oscillating in a swarm, or get an impression of threads and fine stitchwork, to mention 2 of my reactions. A number of pages could be called improvised mandalas.

There aren't any "correct" meanings to read in these pages. Meanings are there for you to find, or reject, as you please. If I'm not mistaken, one of Anneke's intentions is that you reflect on the process of how your mind is dealing with her creations.

Tim Gaze

Mount Barker

June 2017

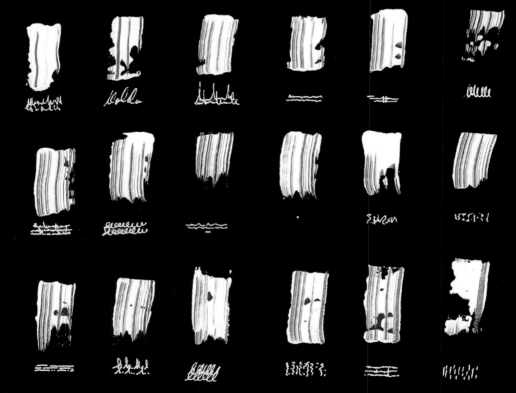

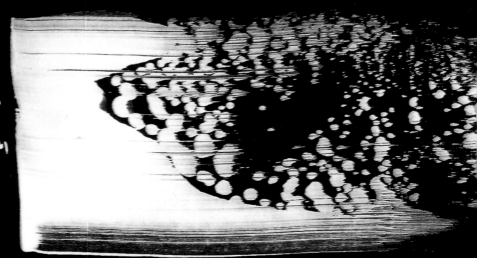

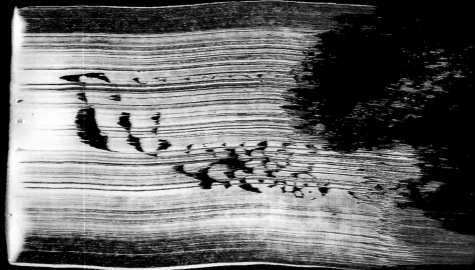

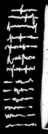
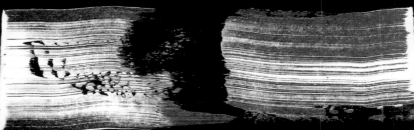

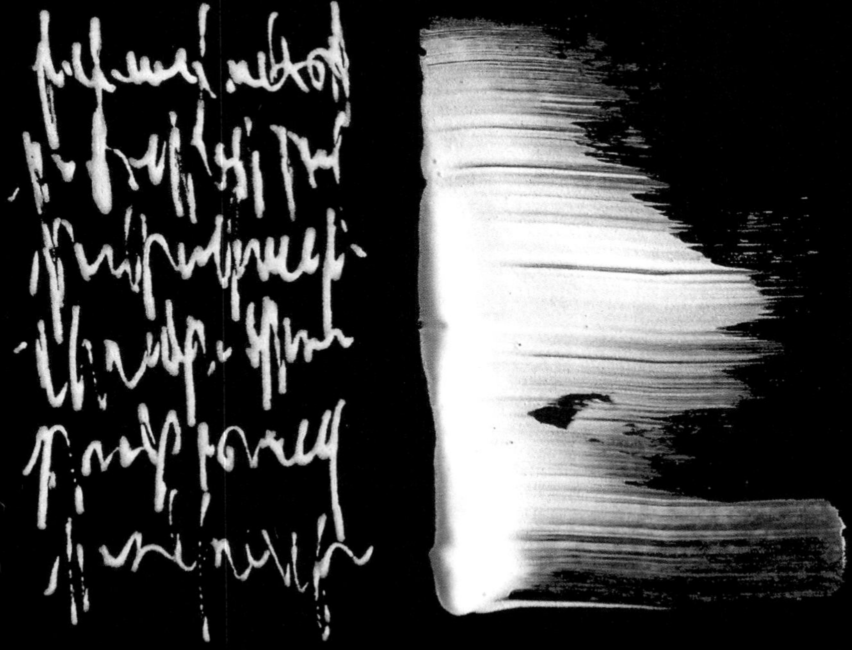

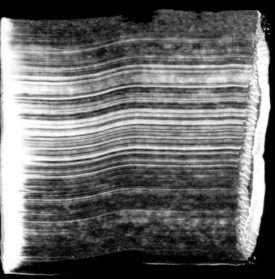

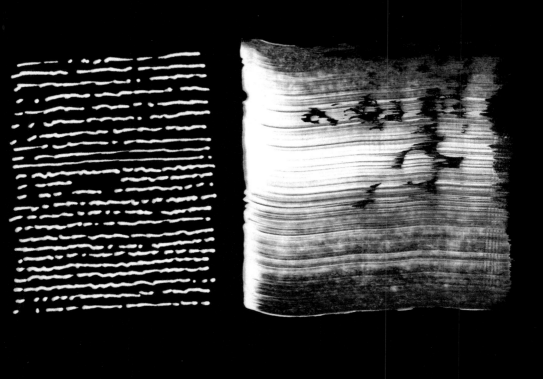

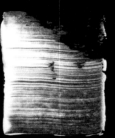

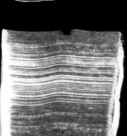

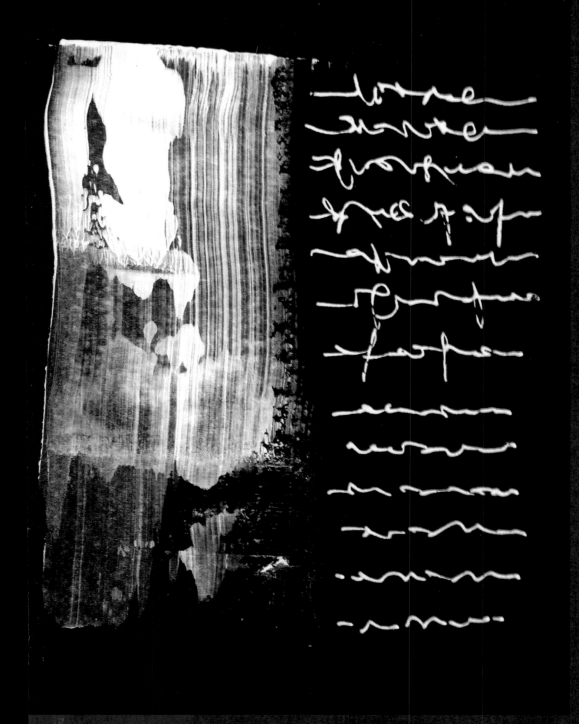

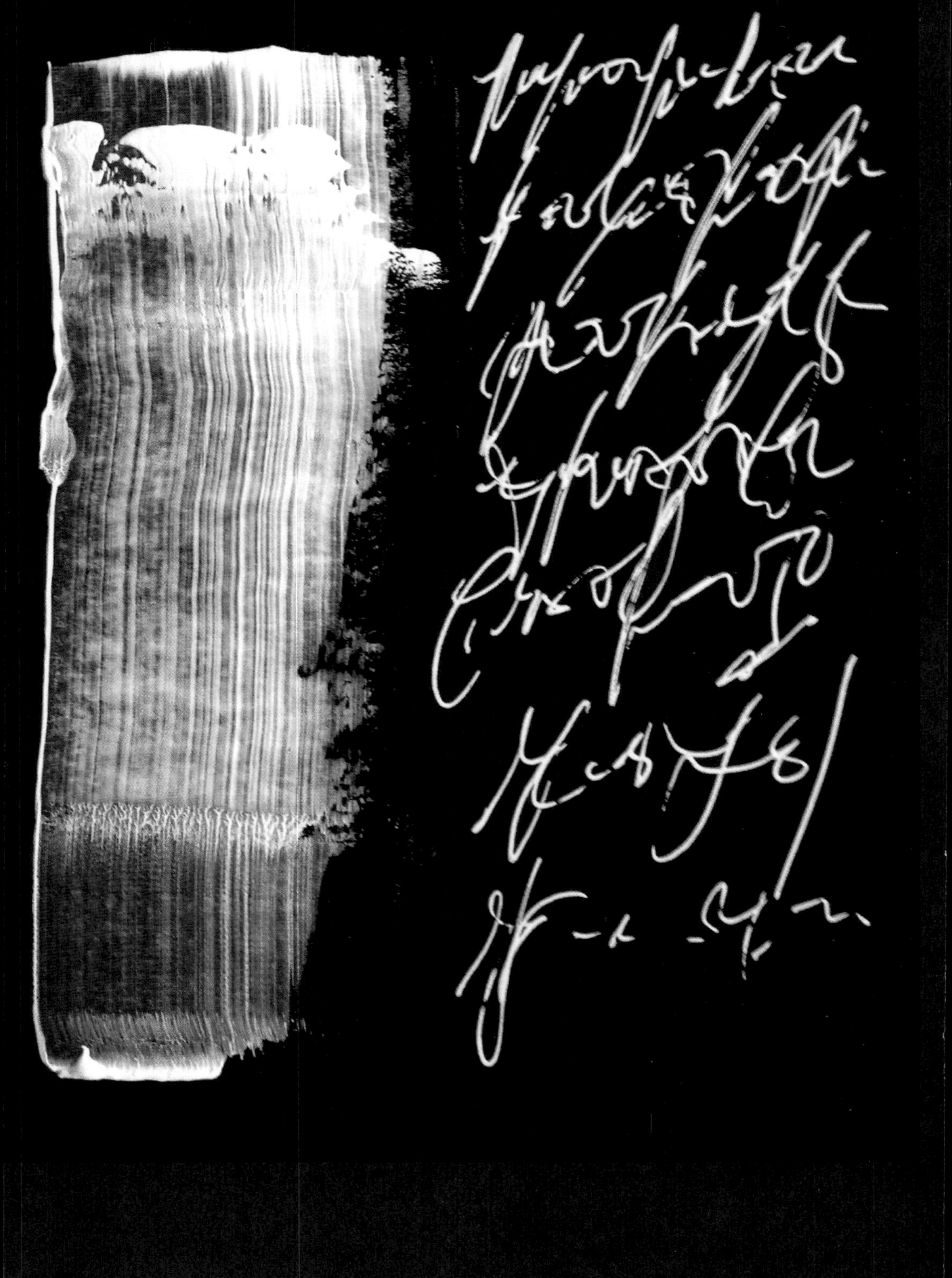

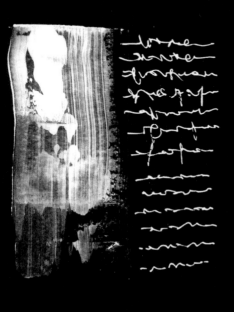

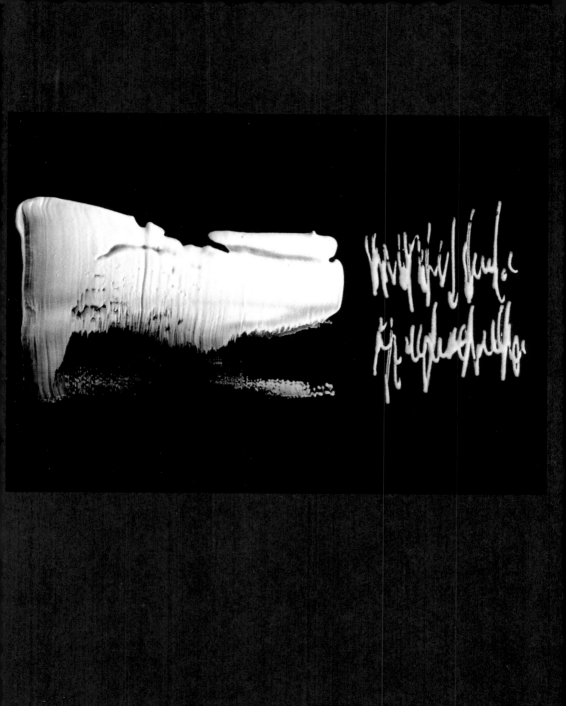

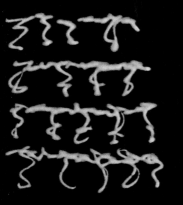

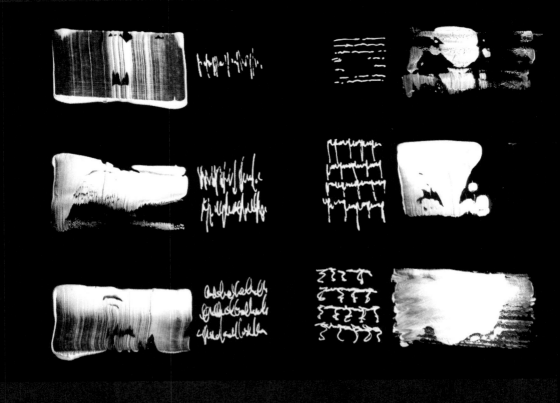

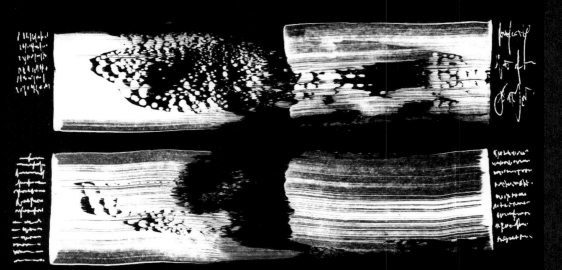

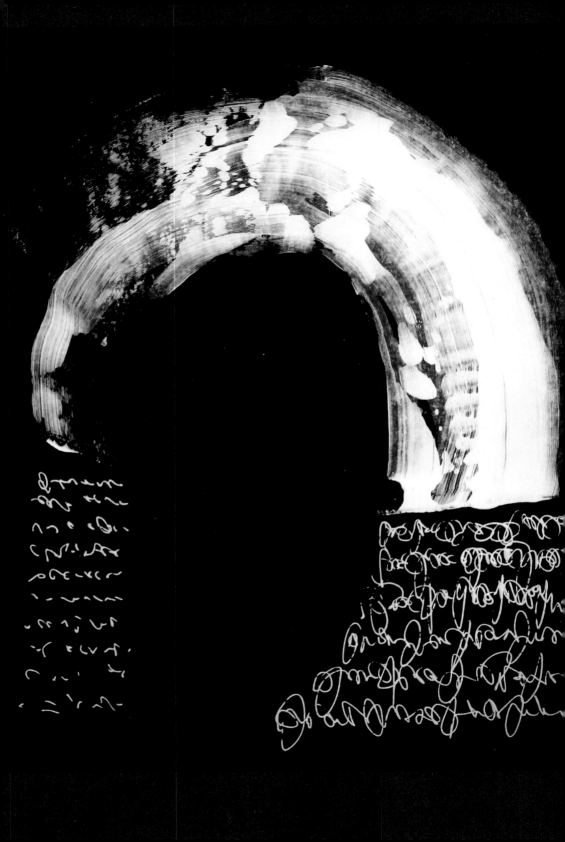

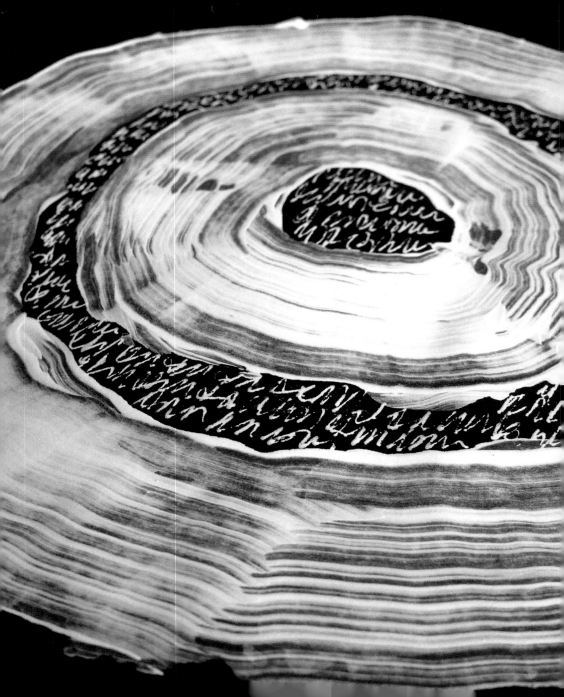

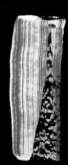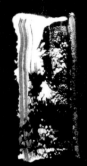
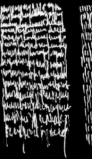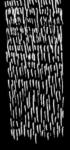

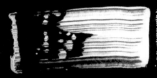

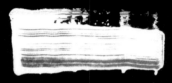

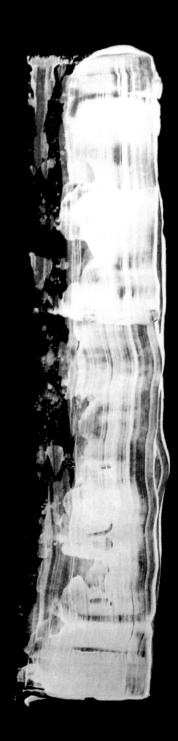

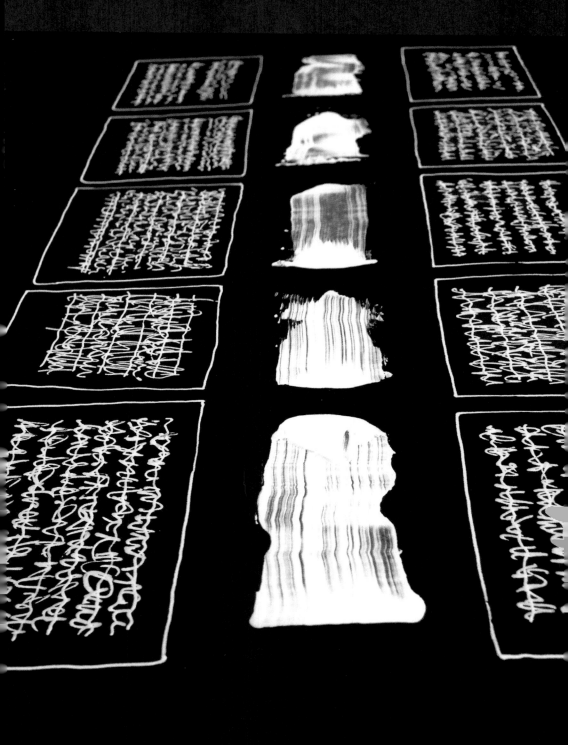

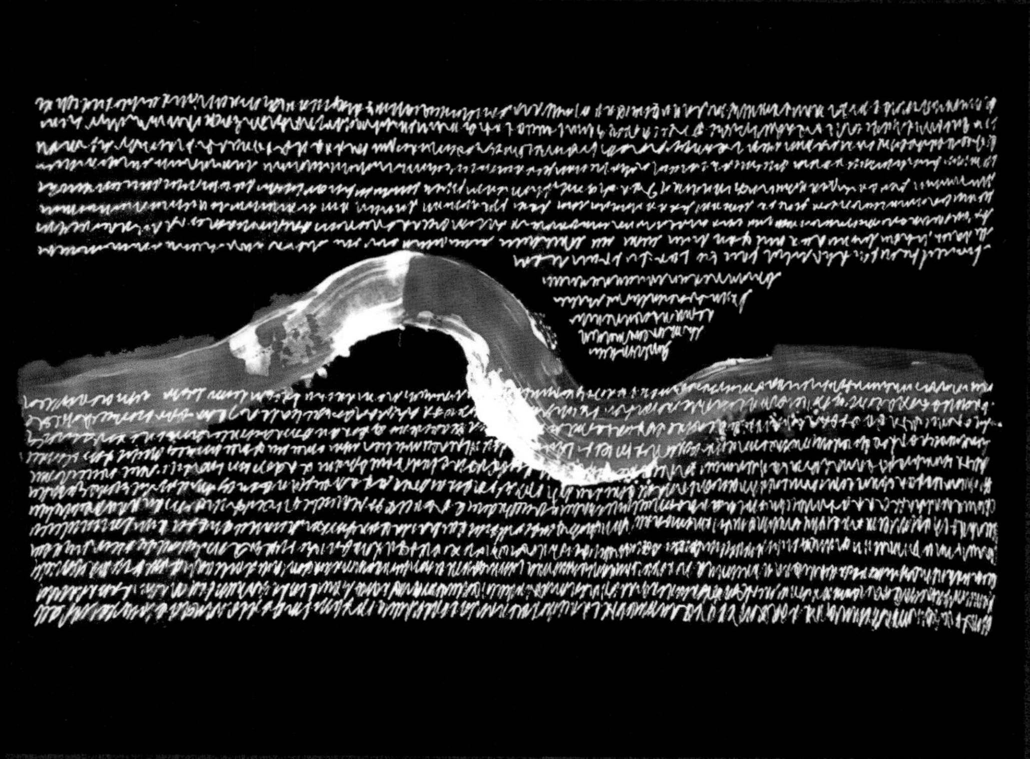

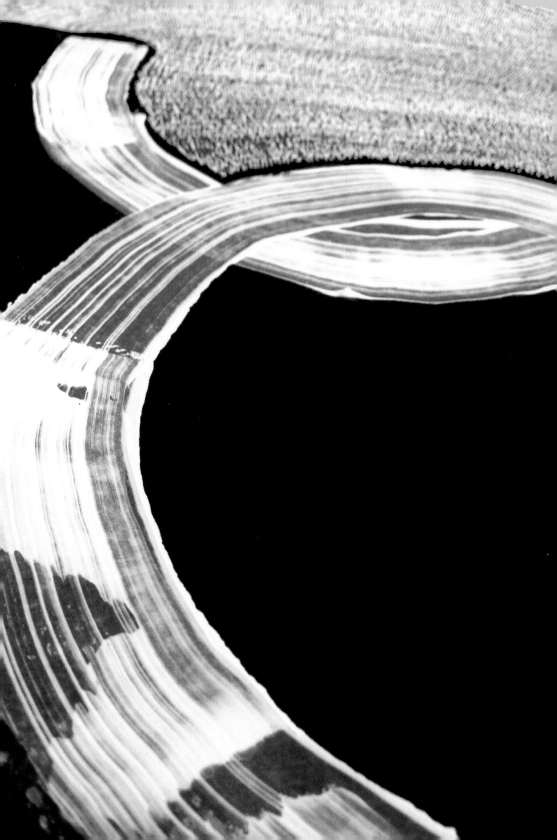

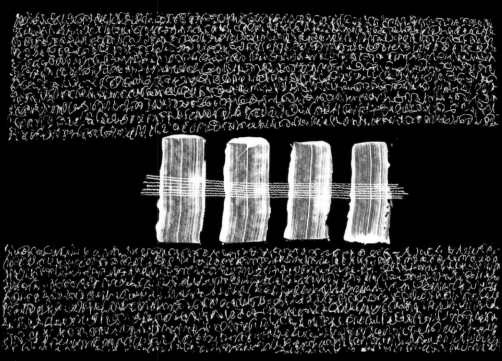

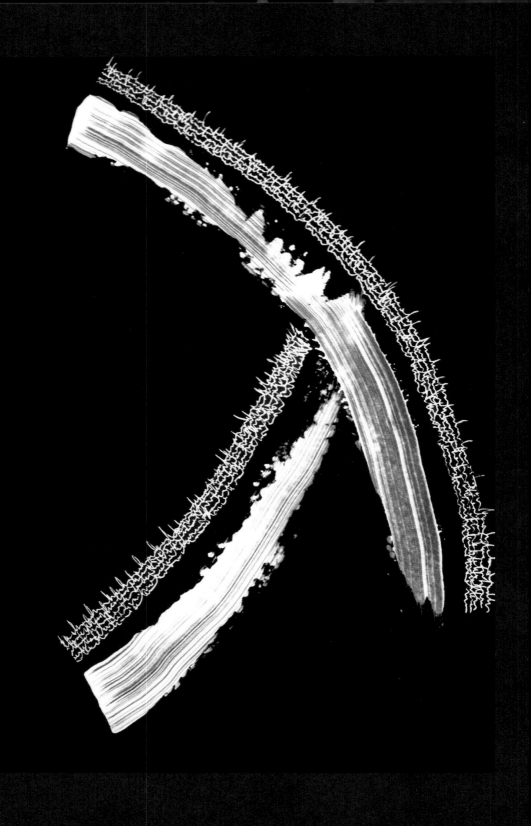

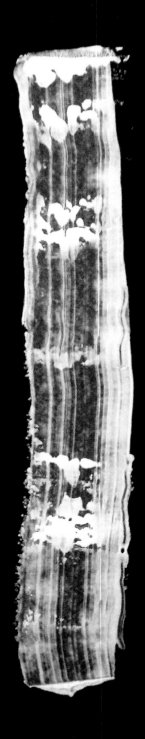

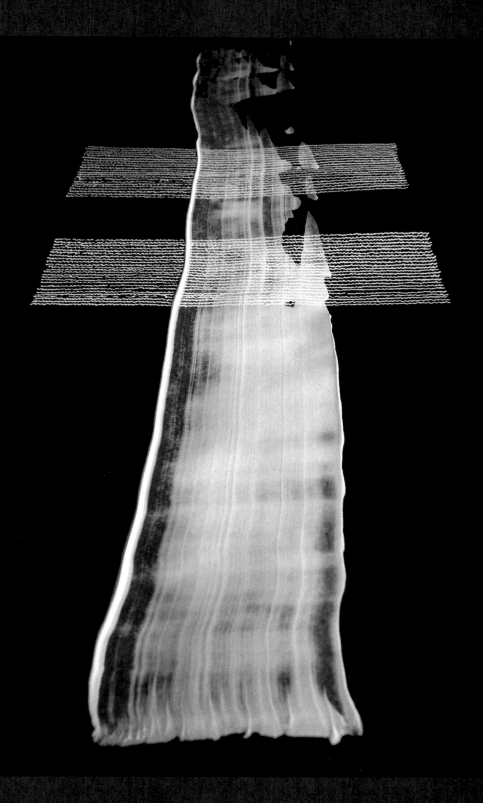

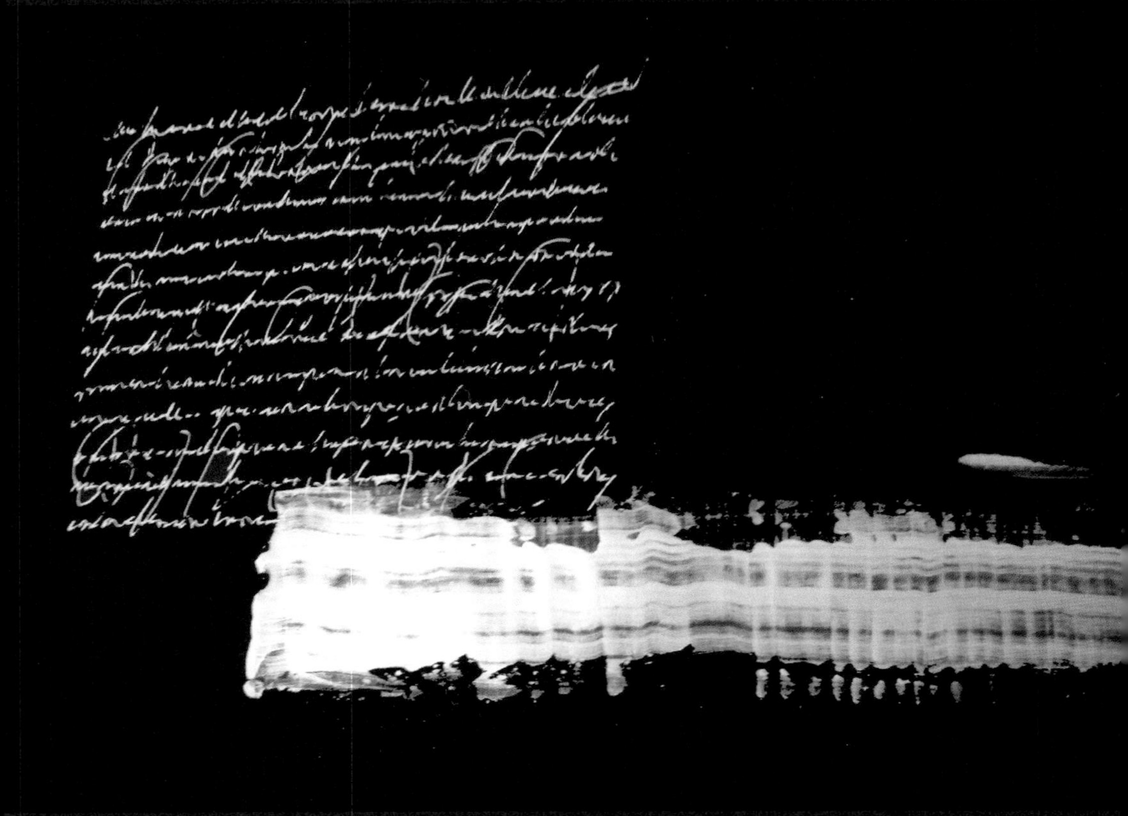

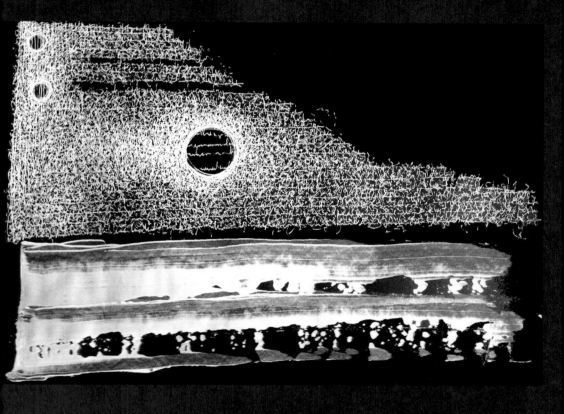

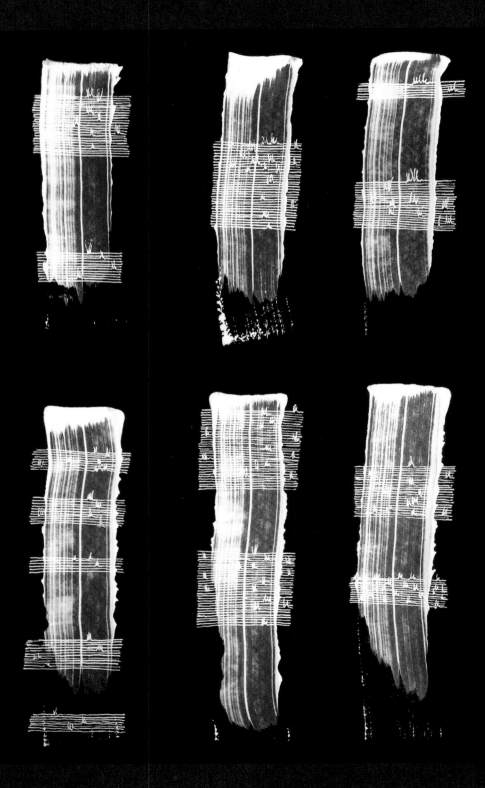

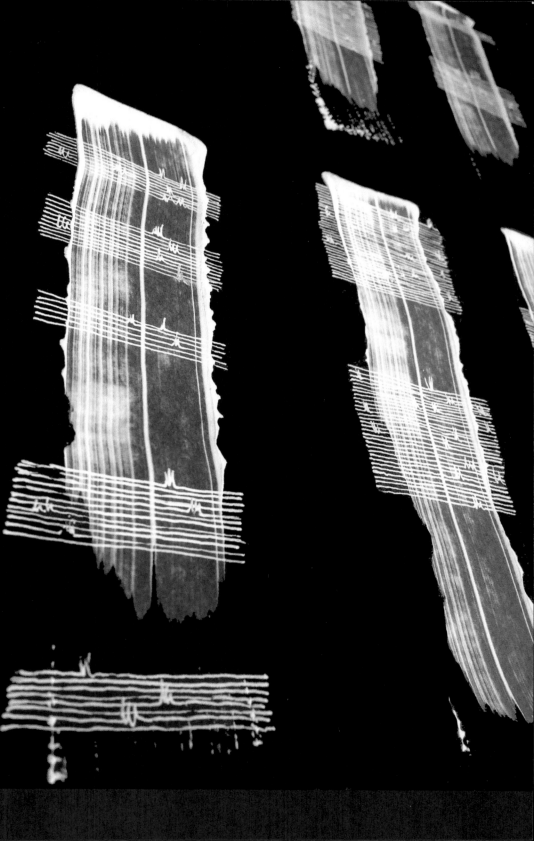

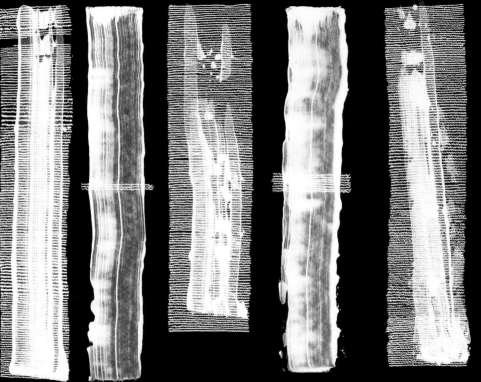

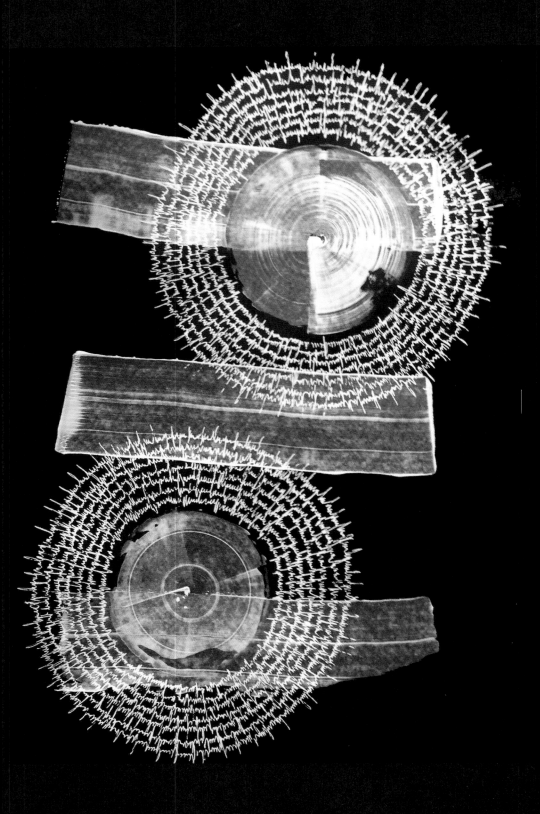

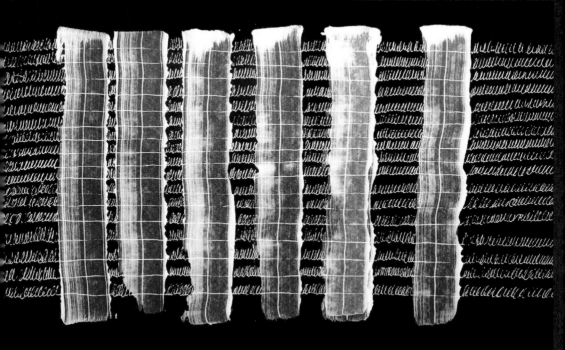

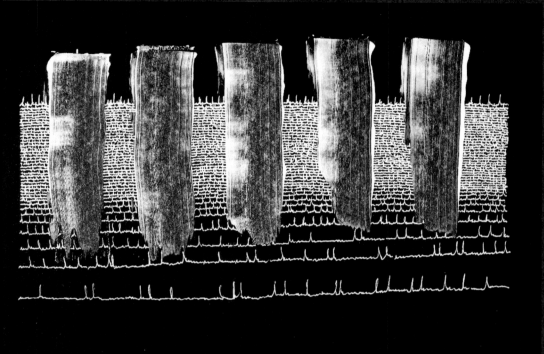

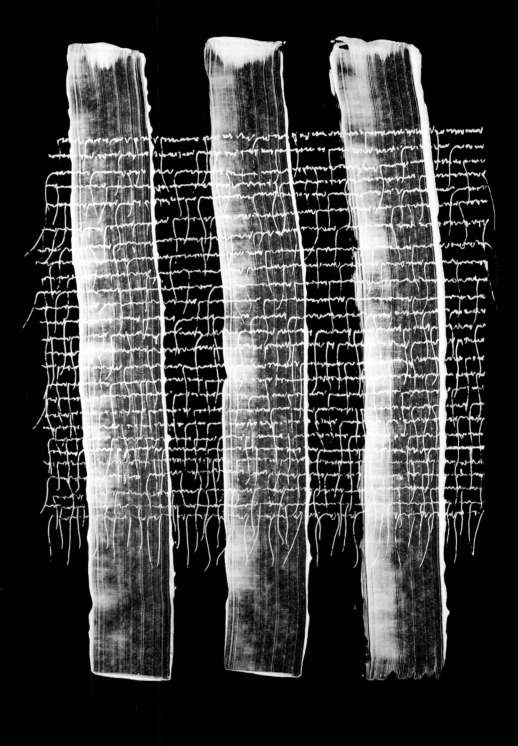

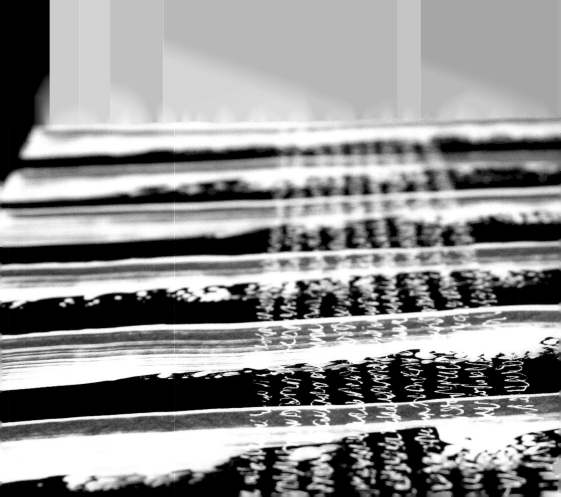

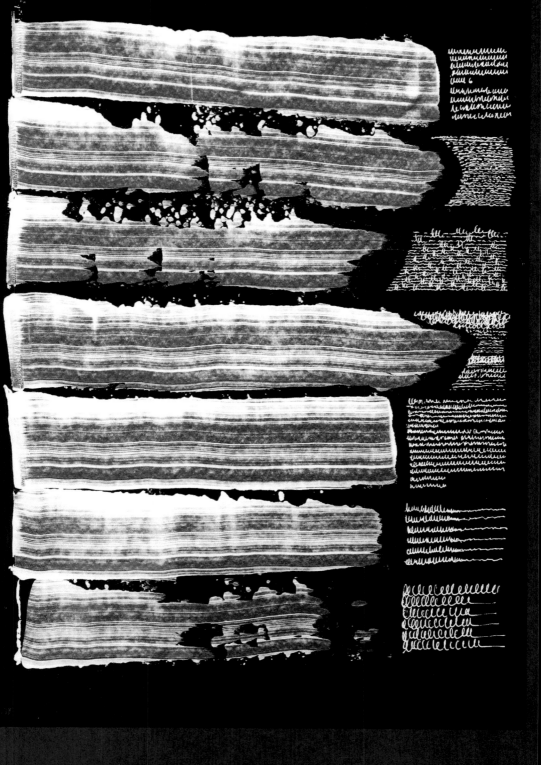

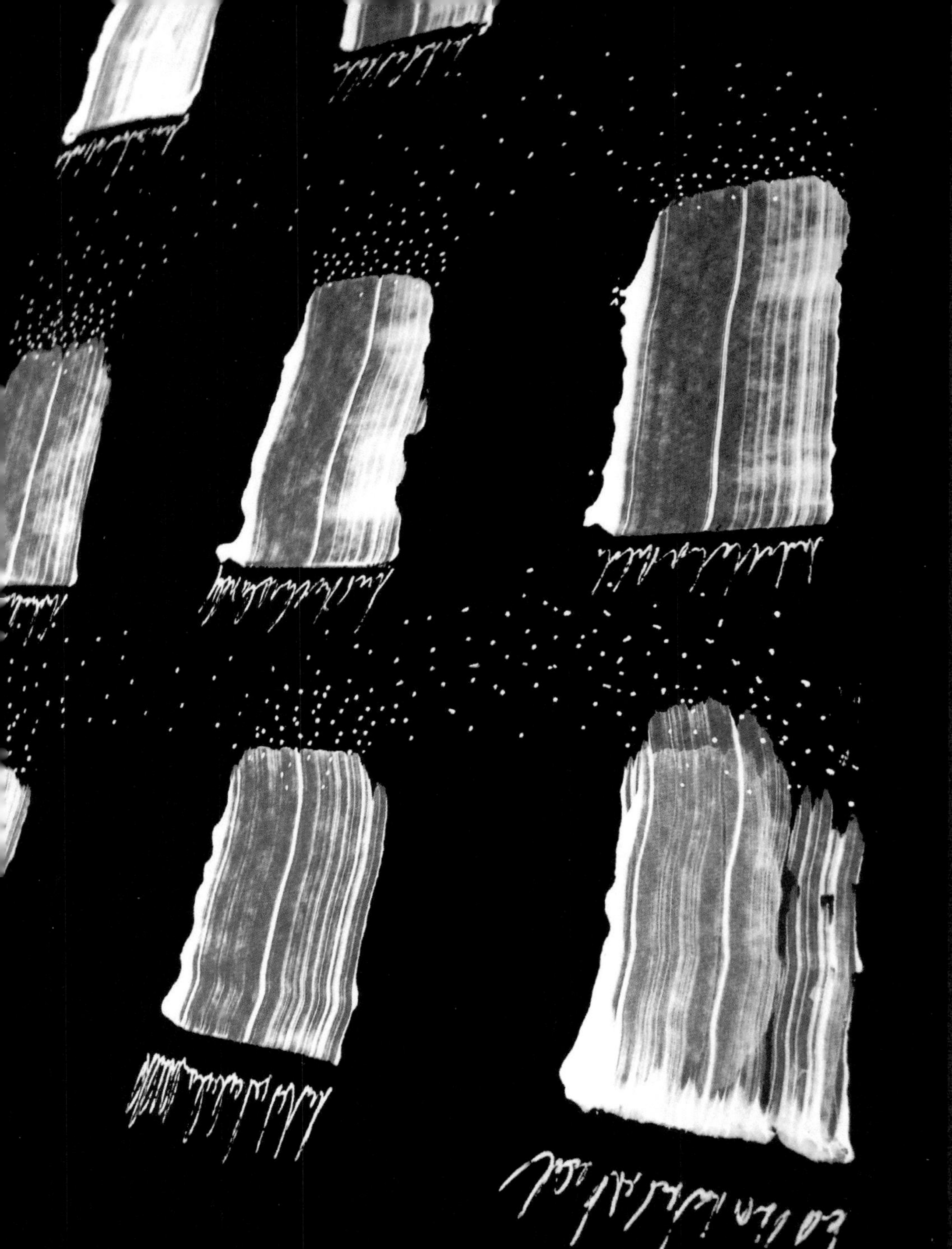

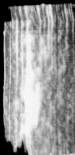

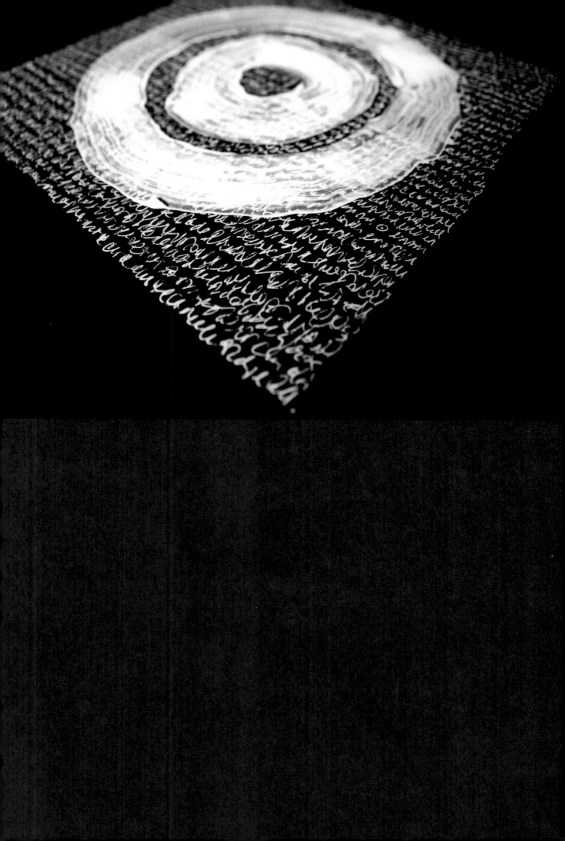

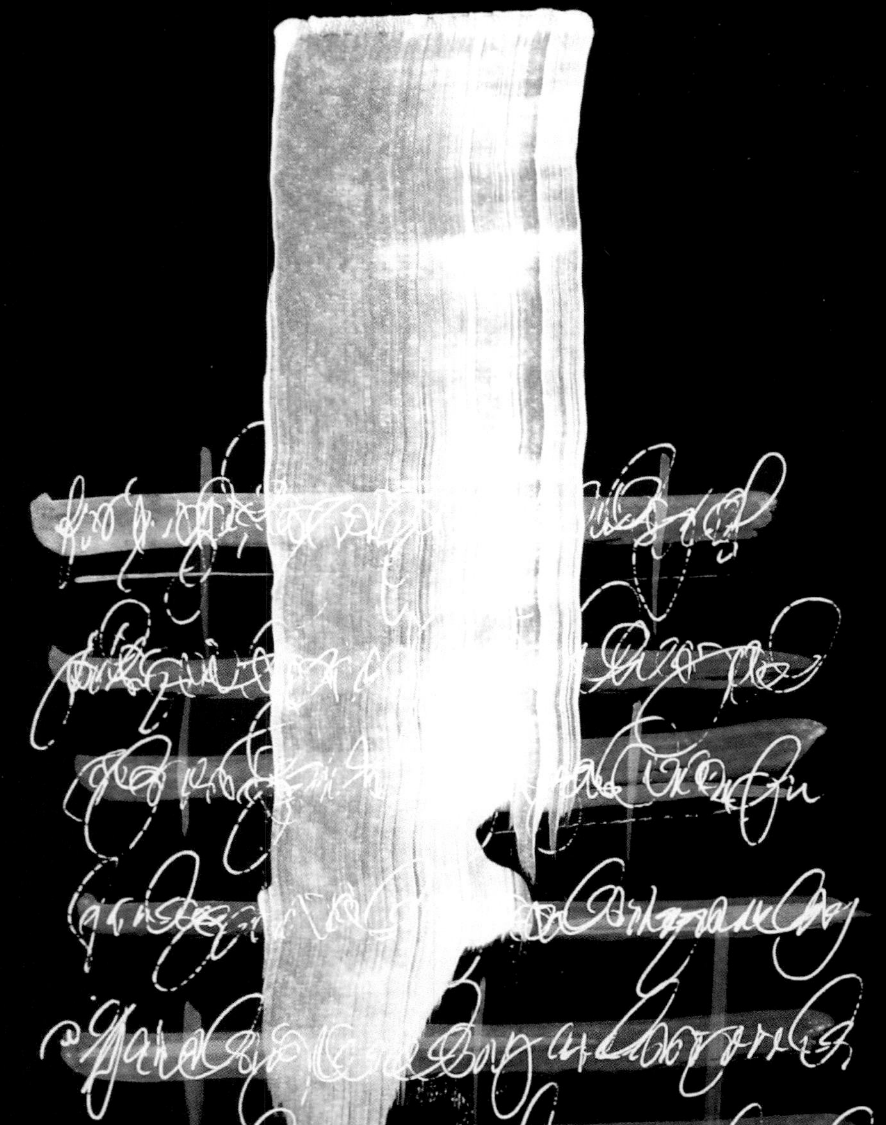

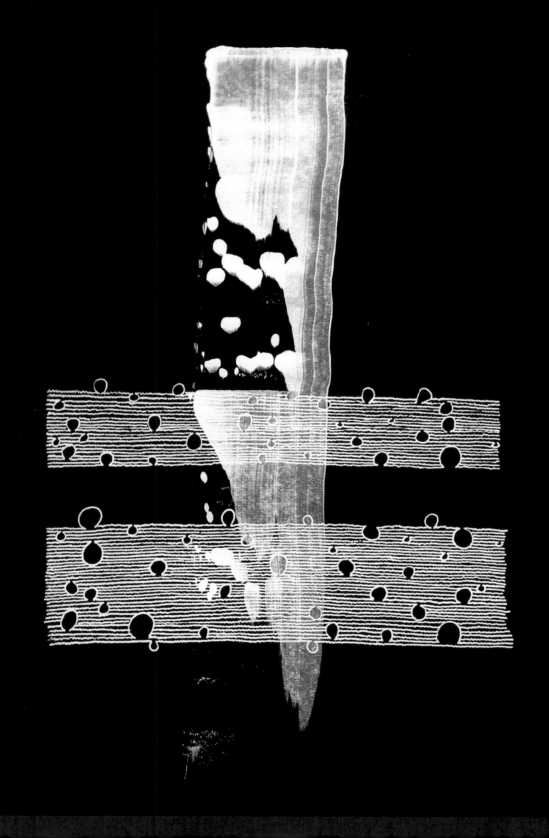

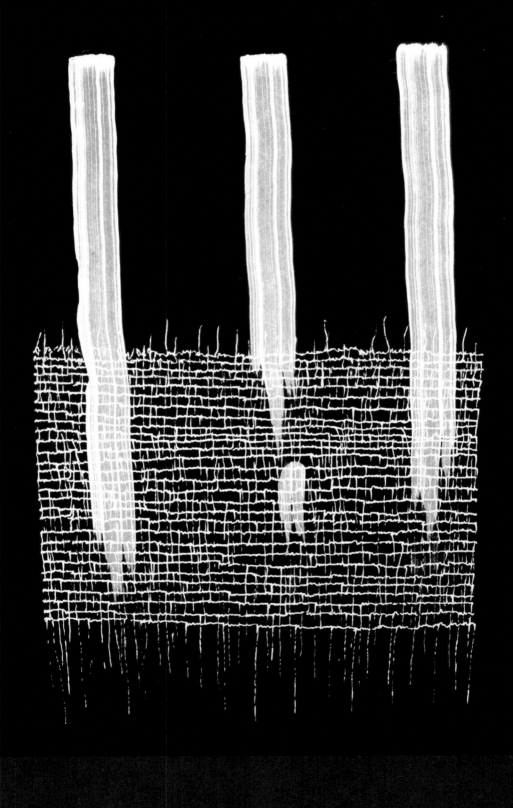

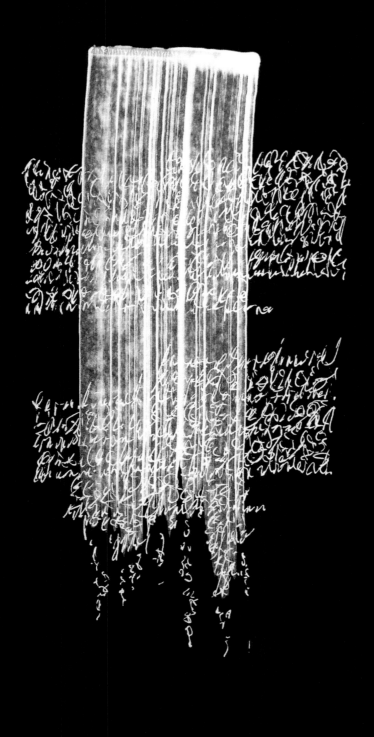

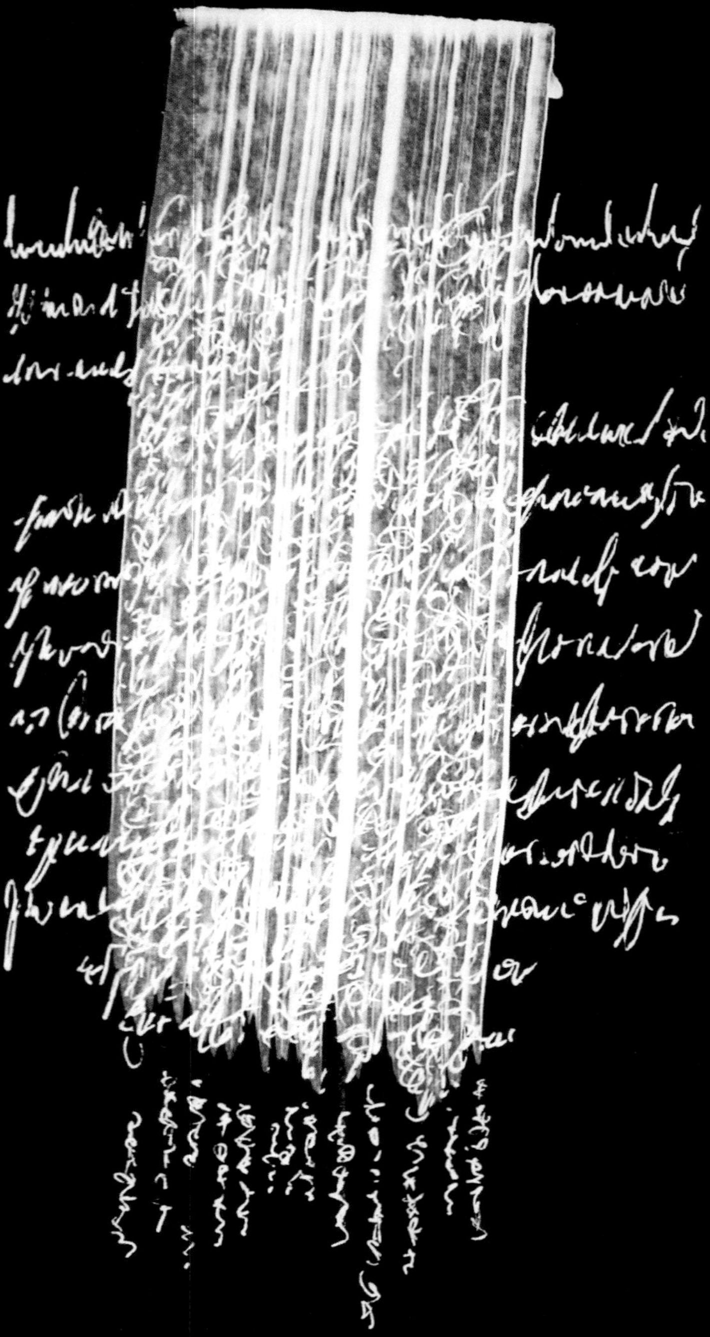

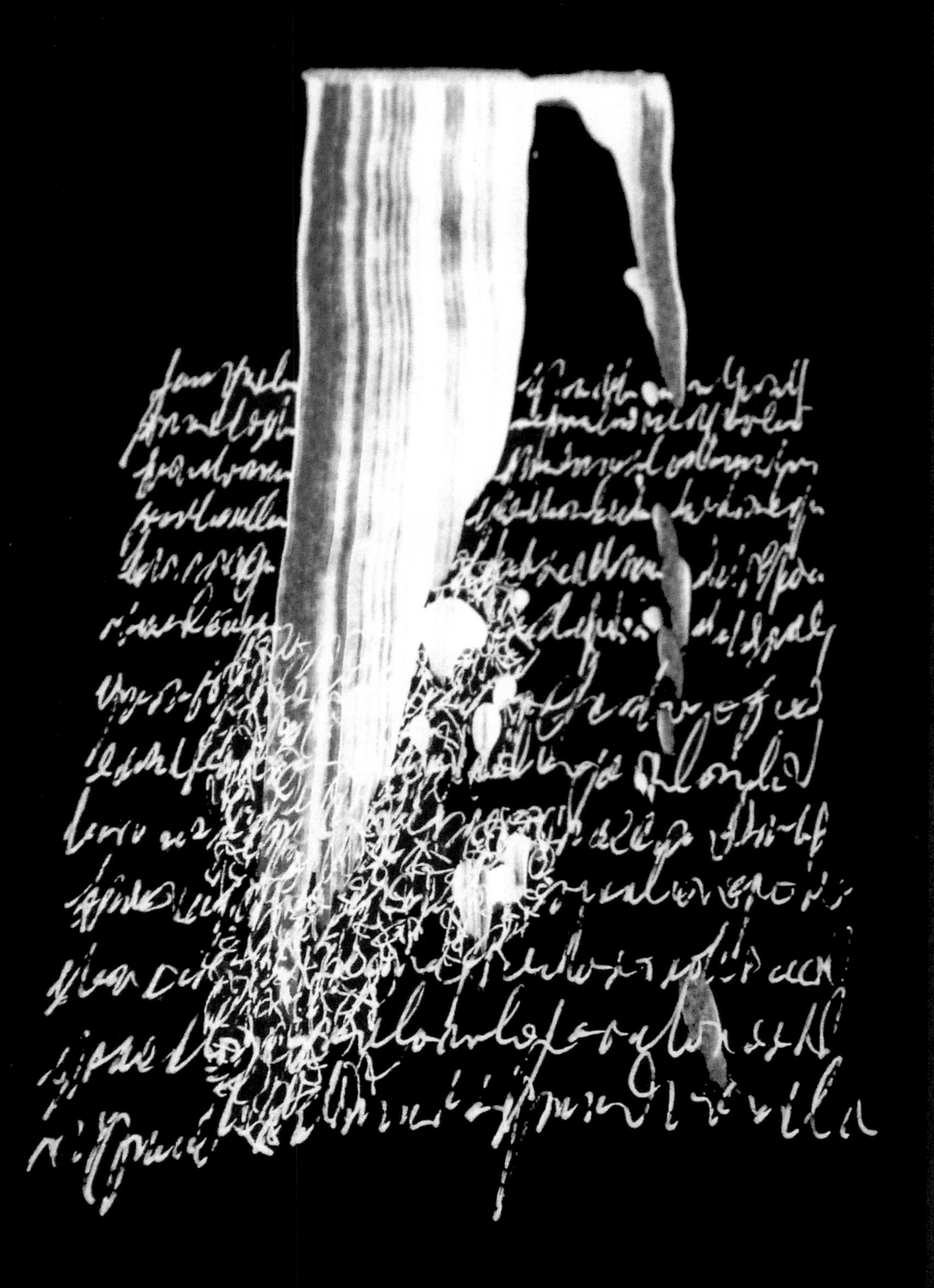

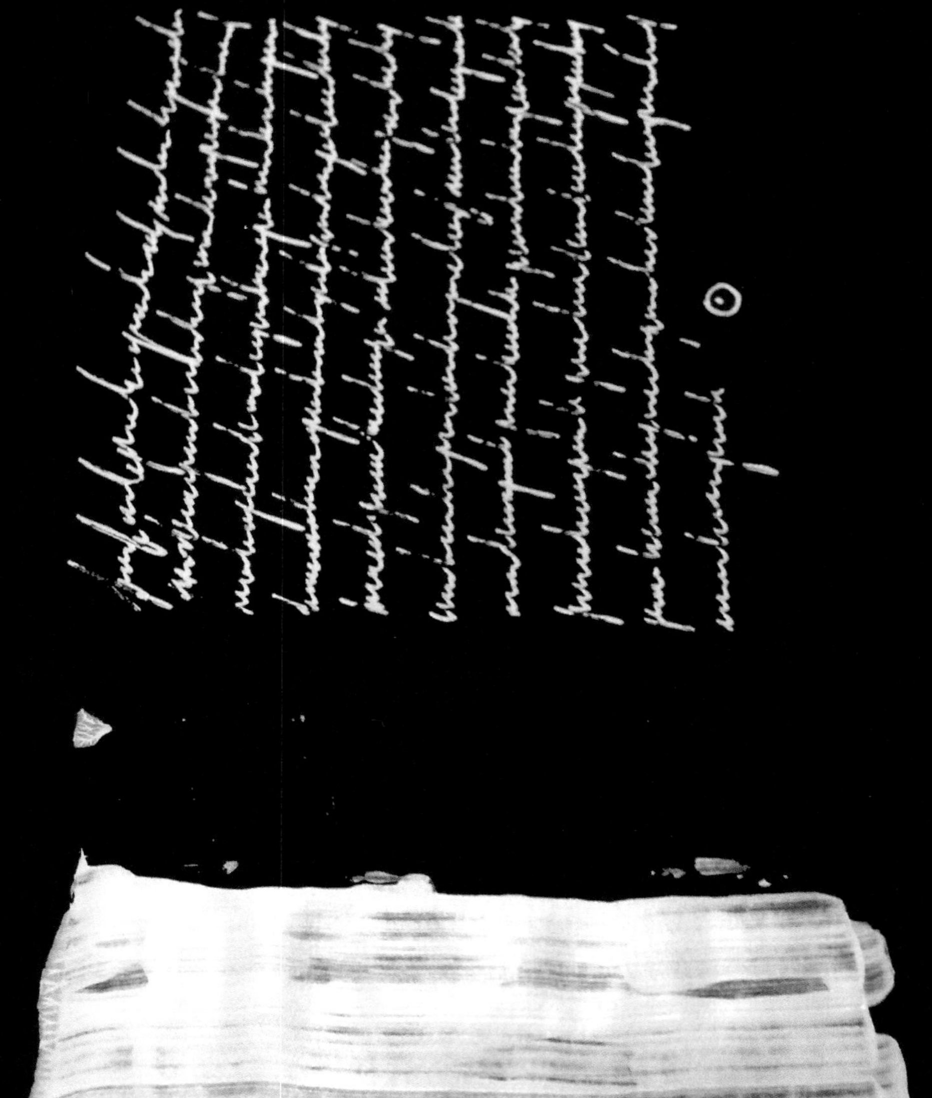

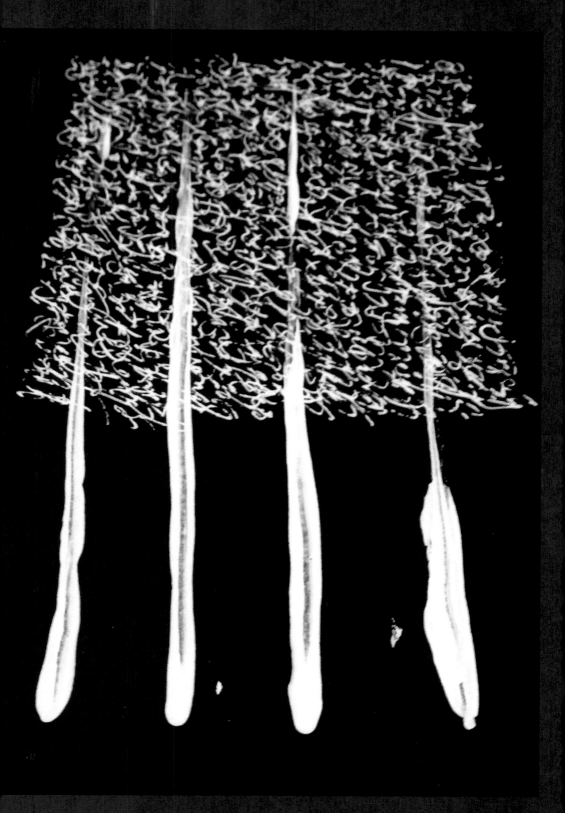

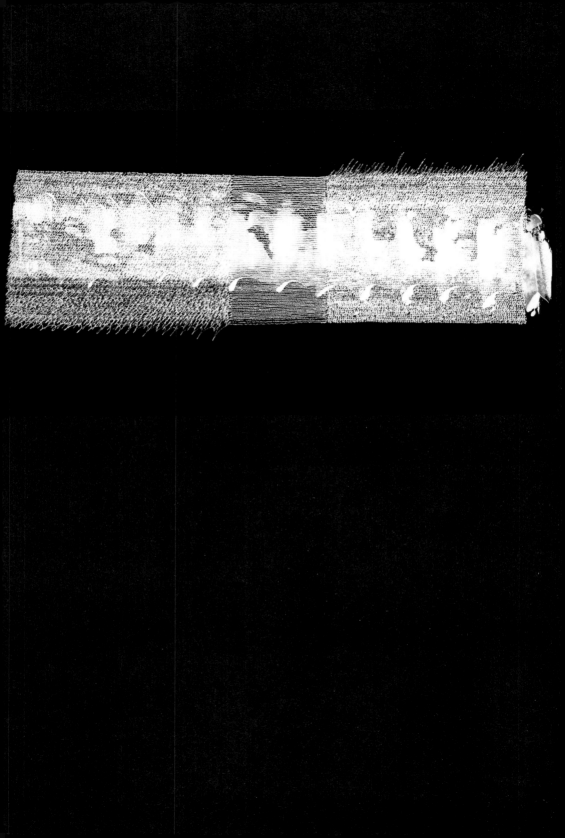

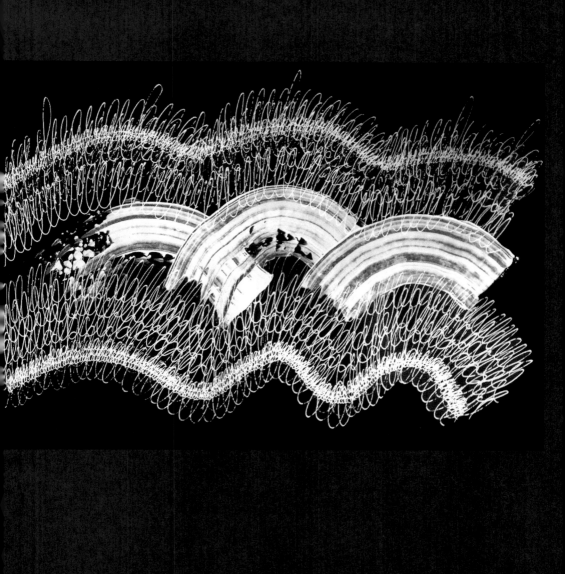

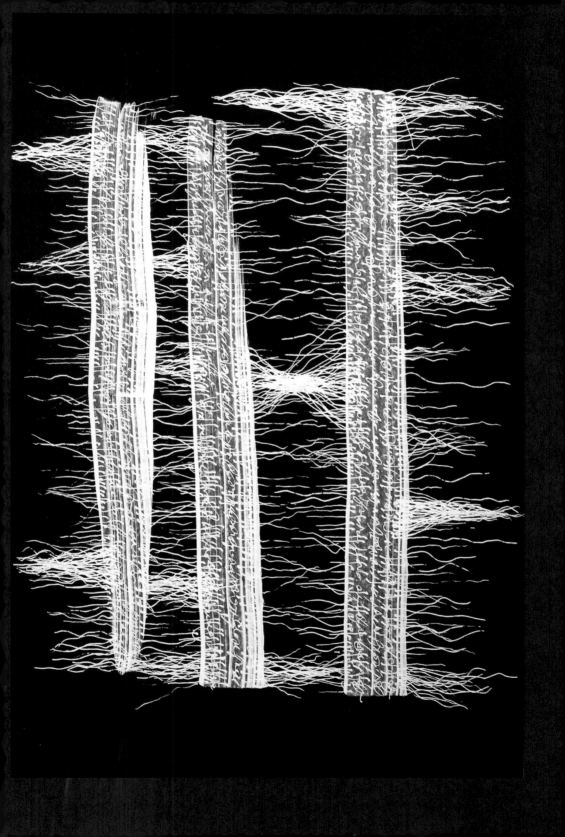

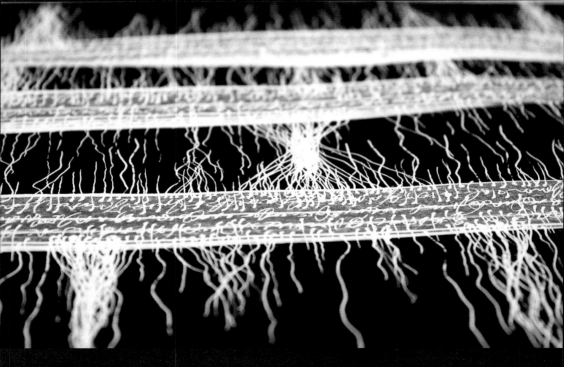

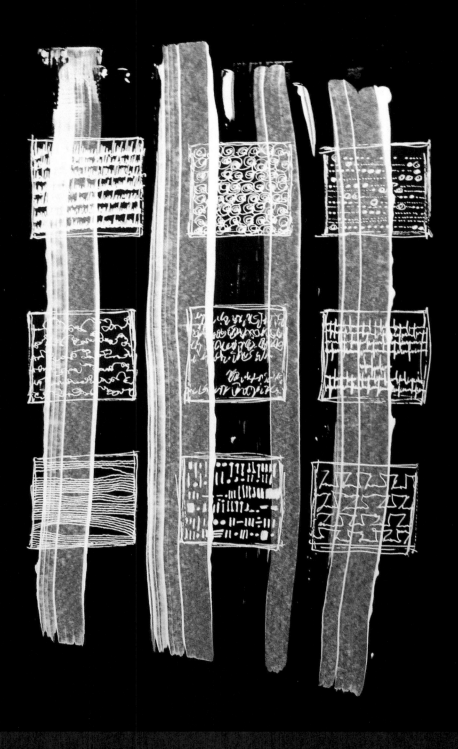

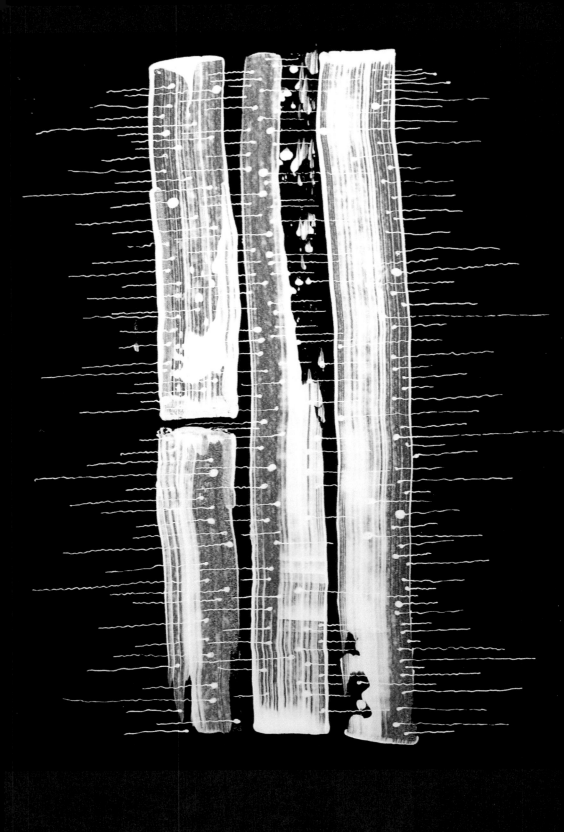

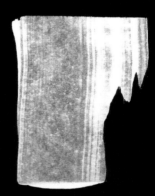

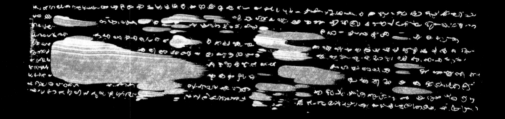

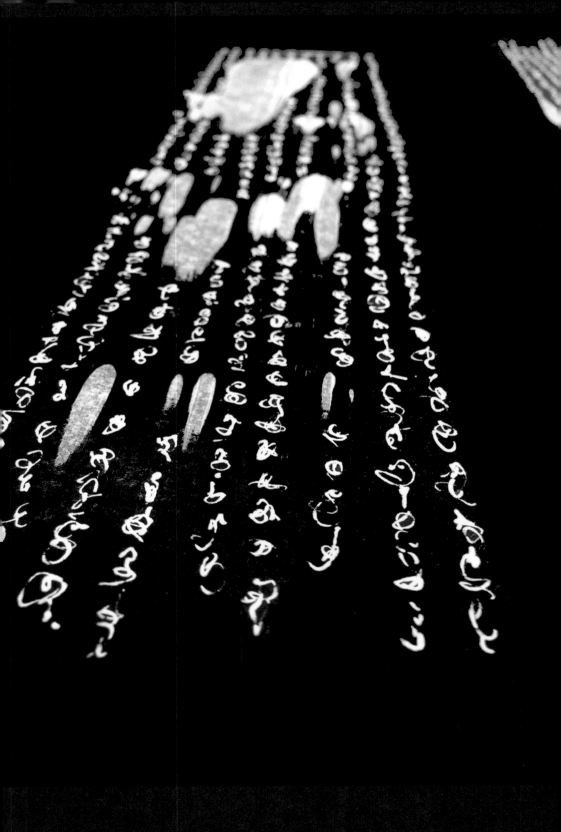

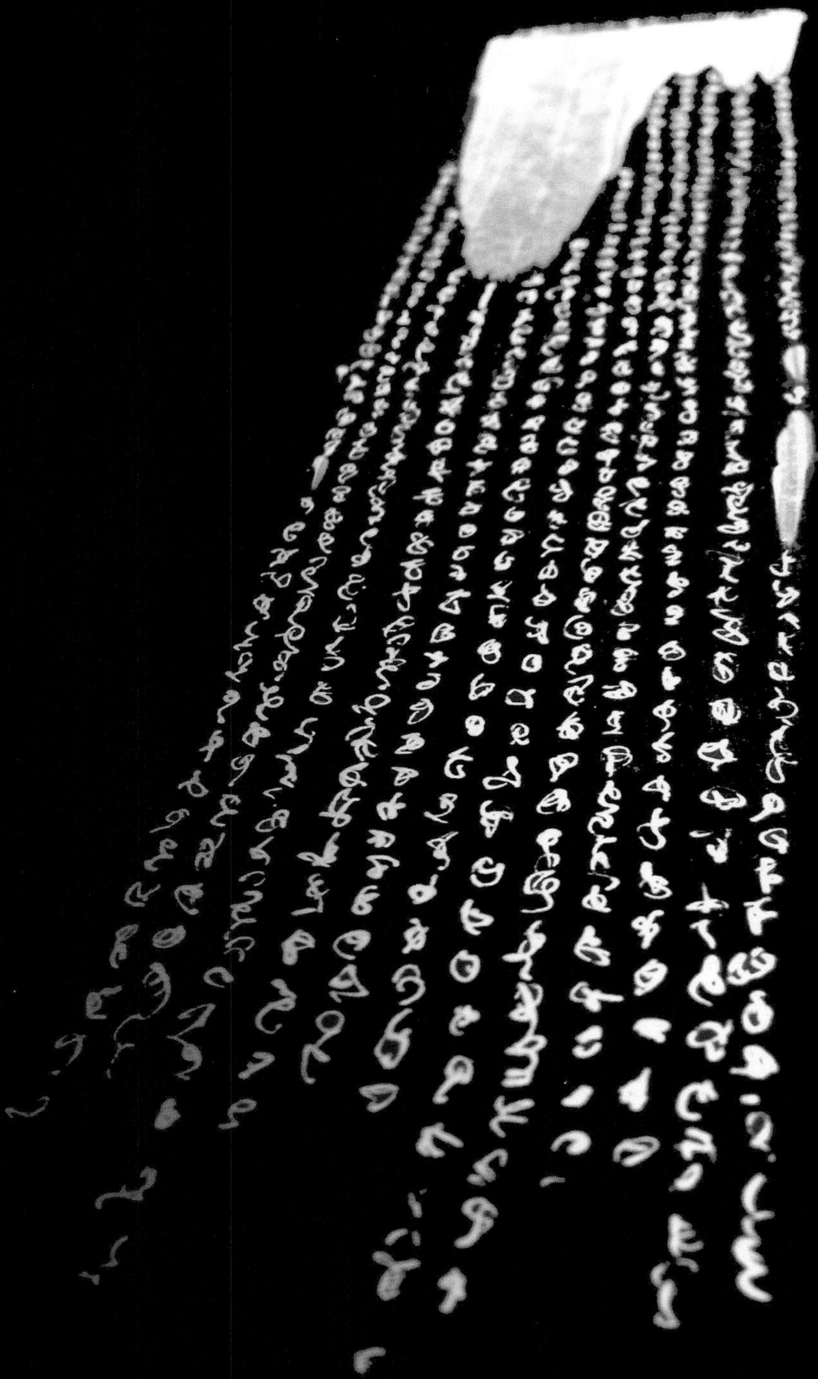

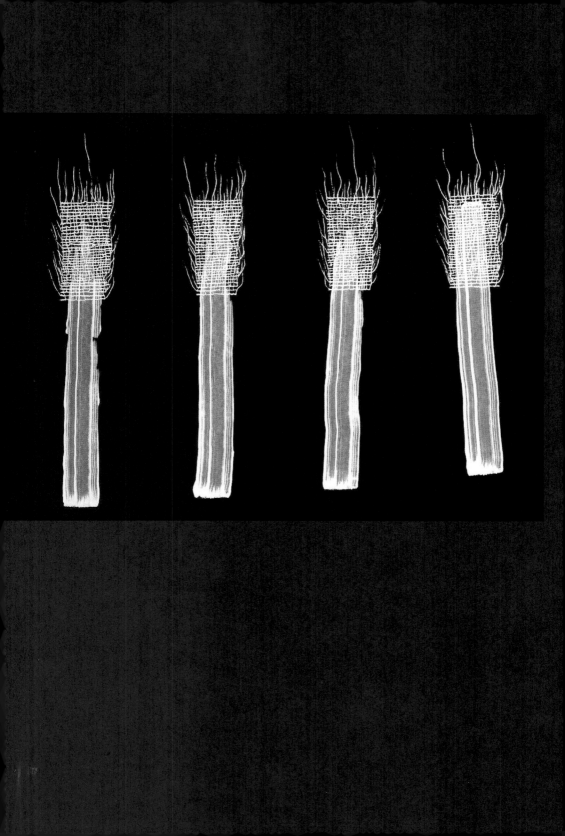

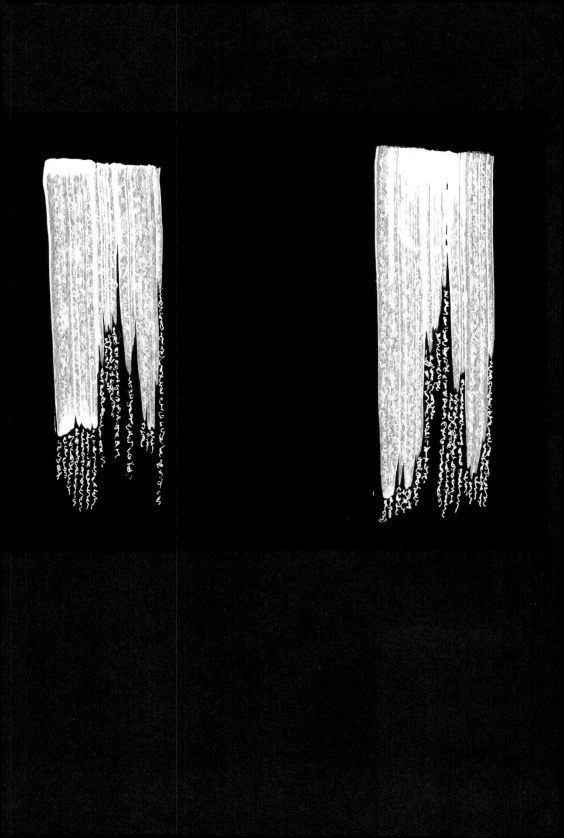

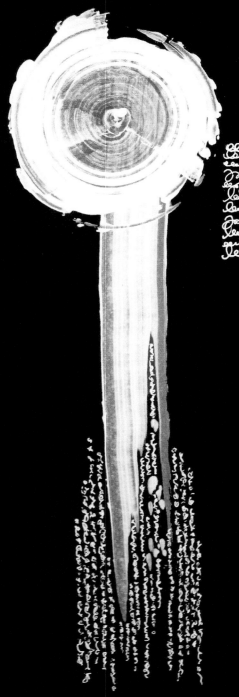

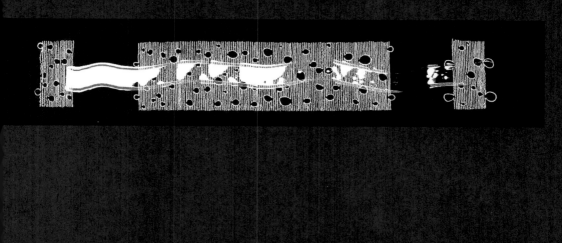

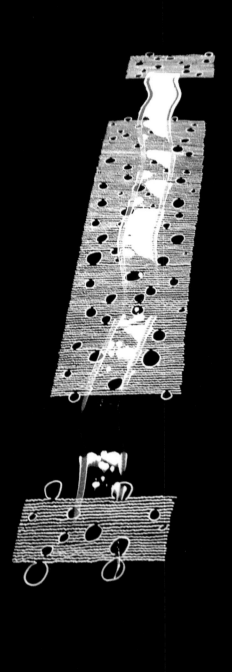
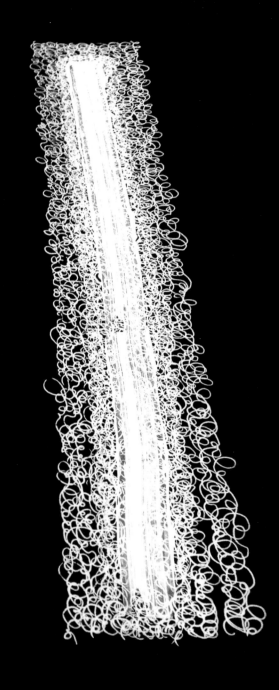

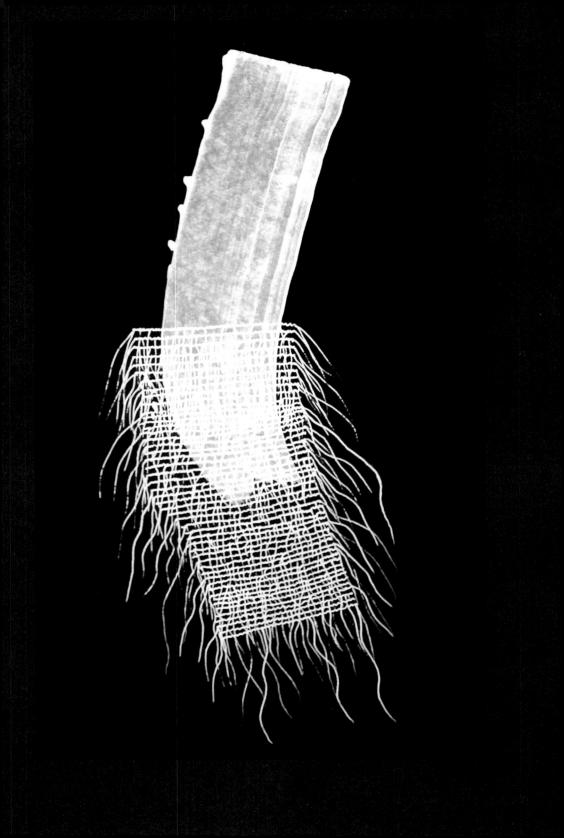

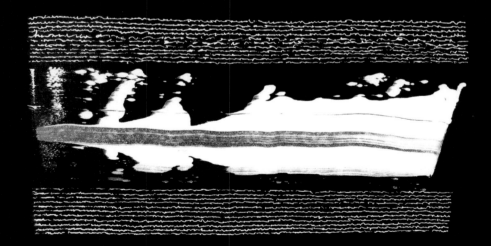

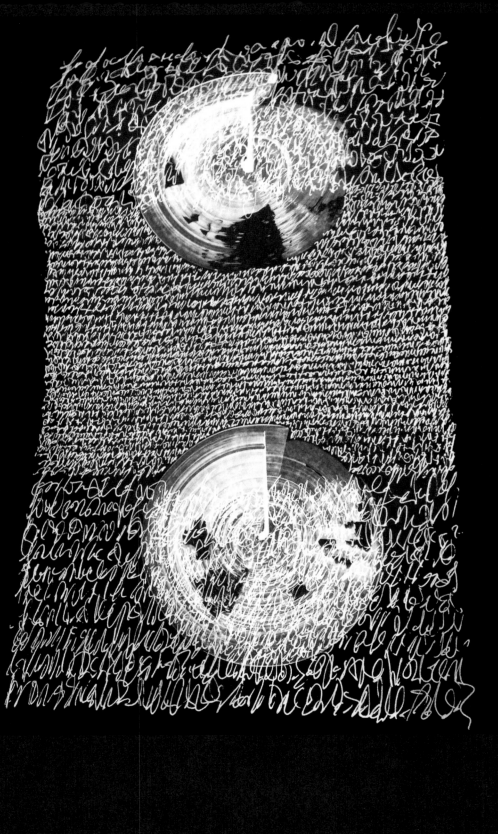

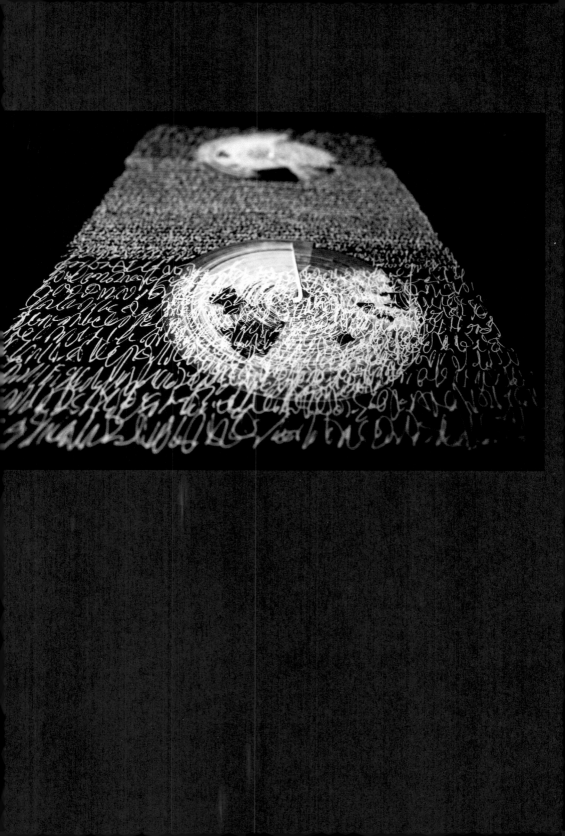

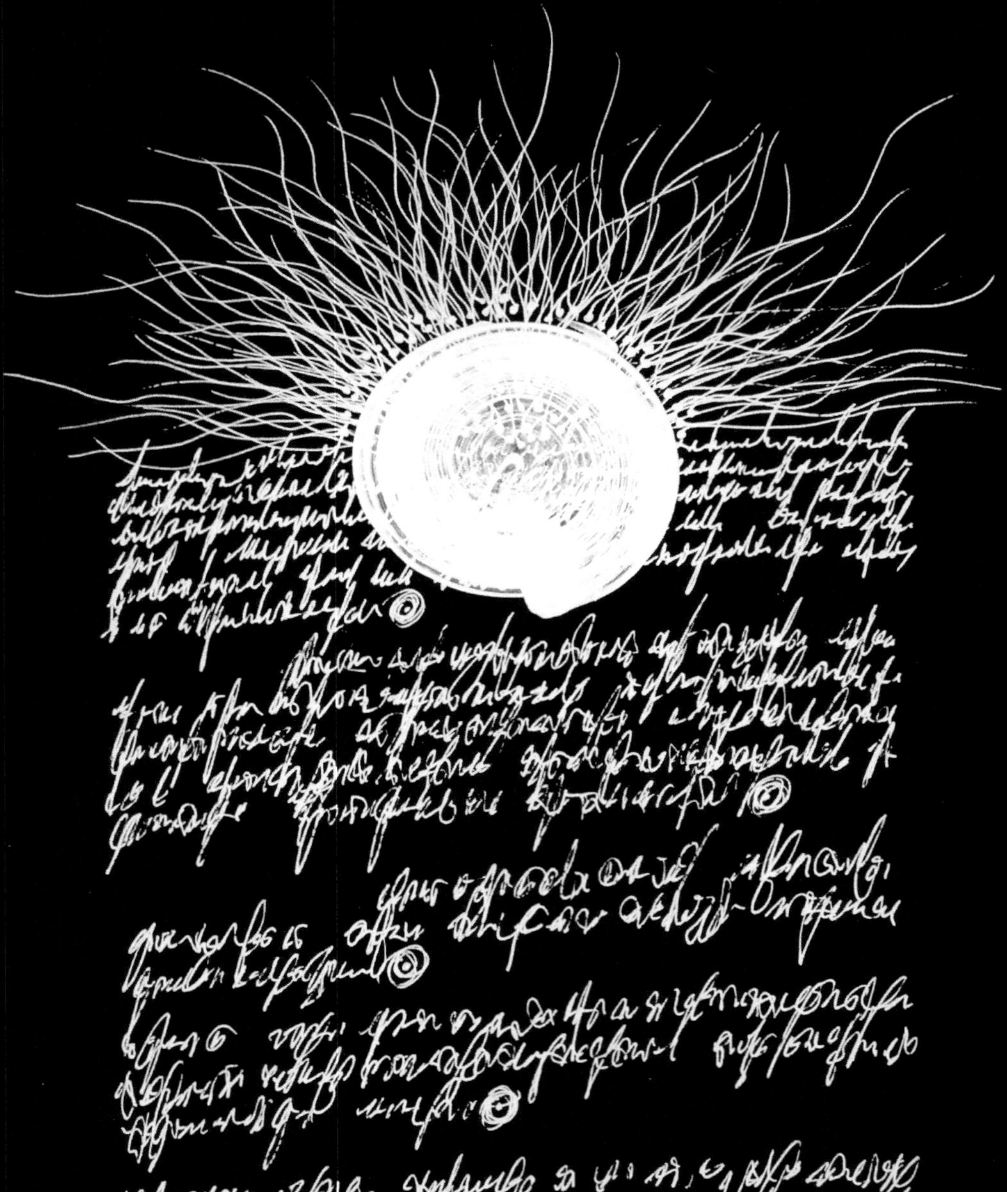

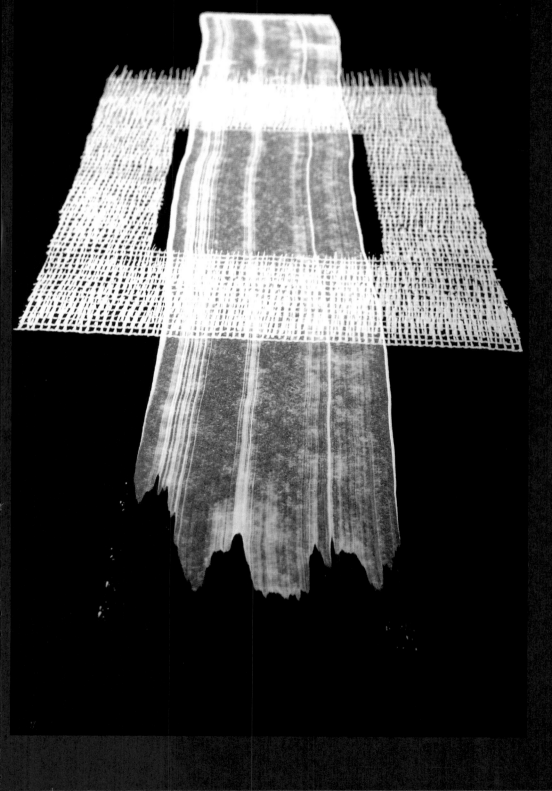

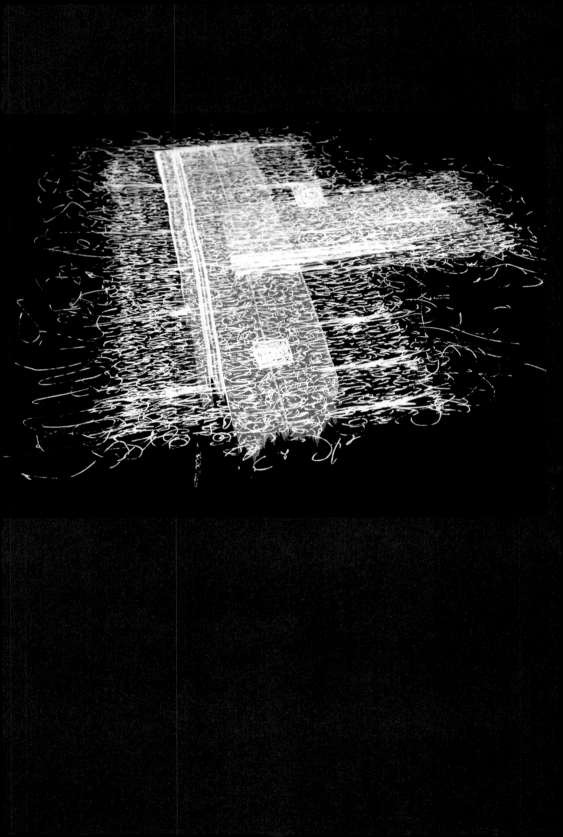

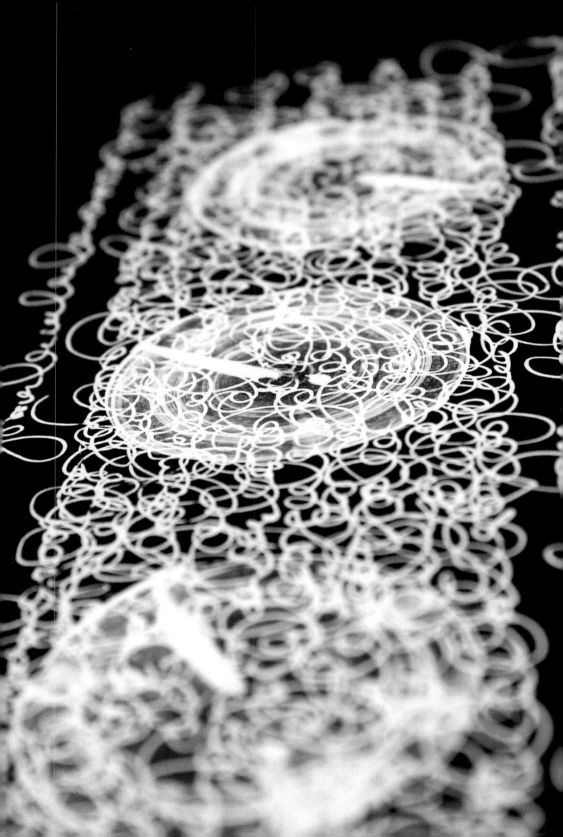

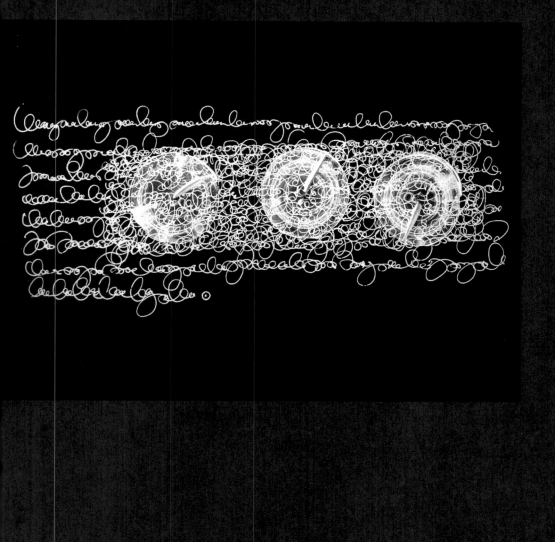

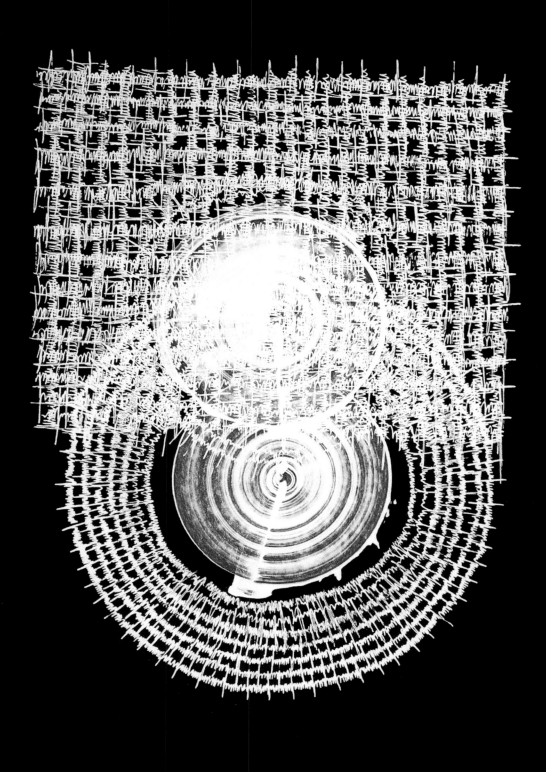

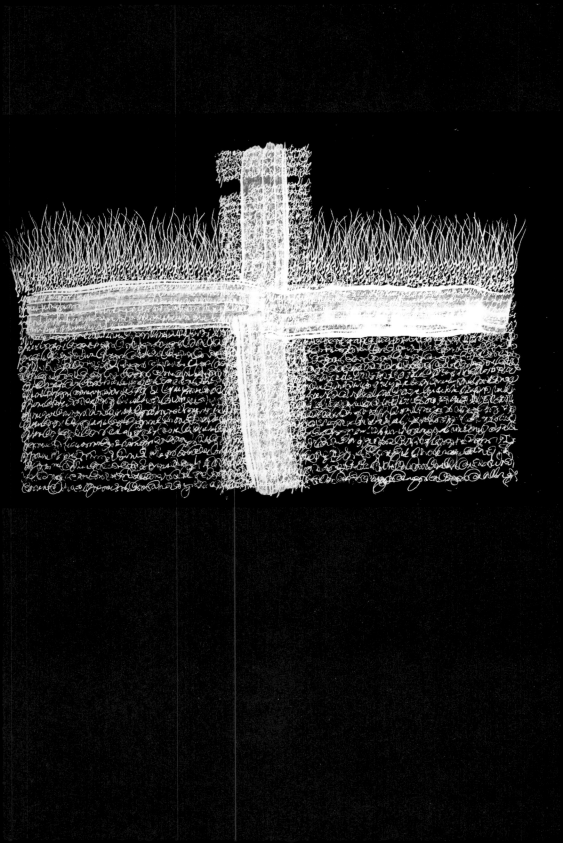

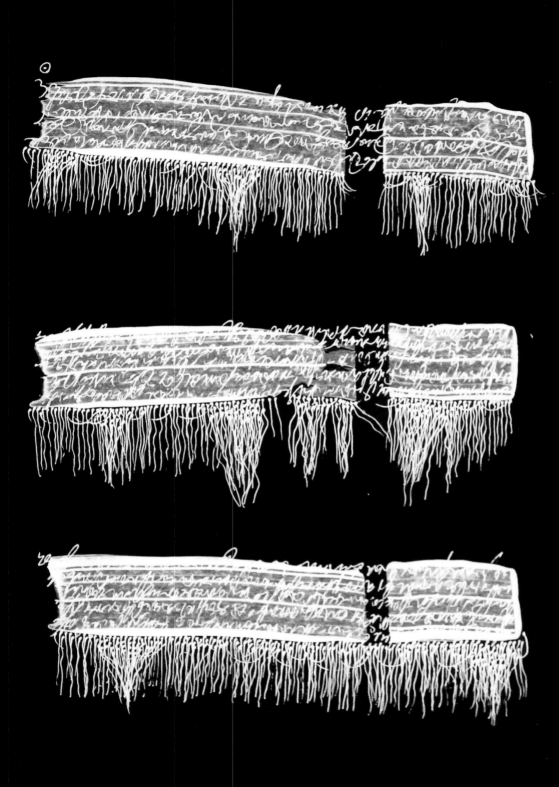

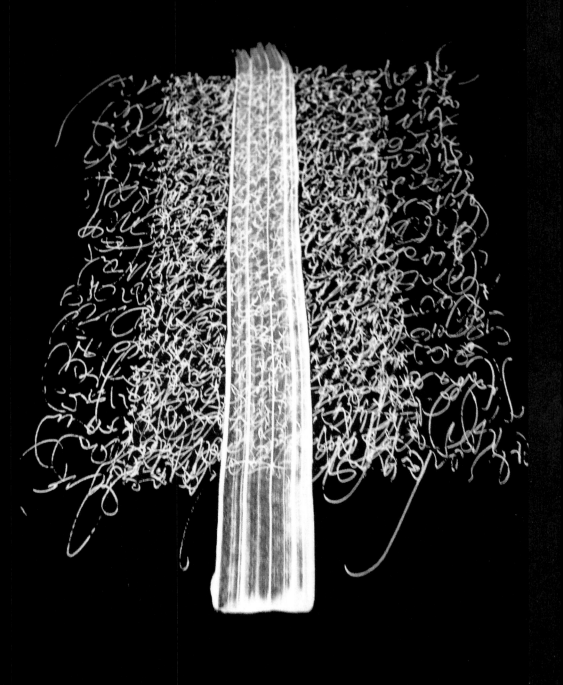

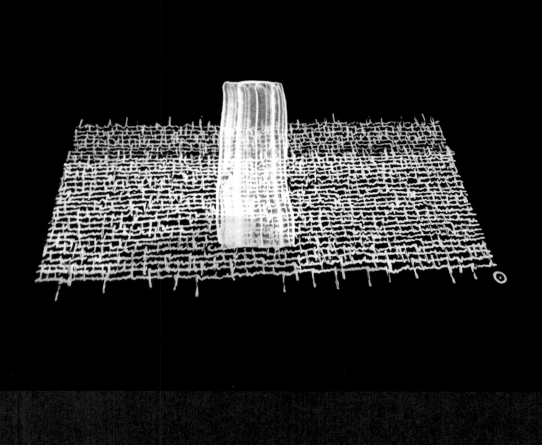

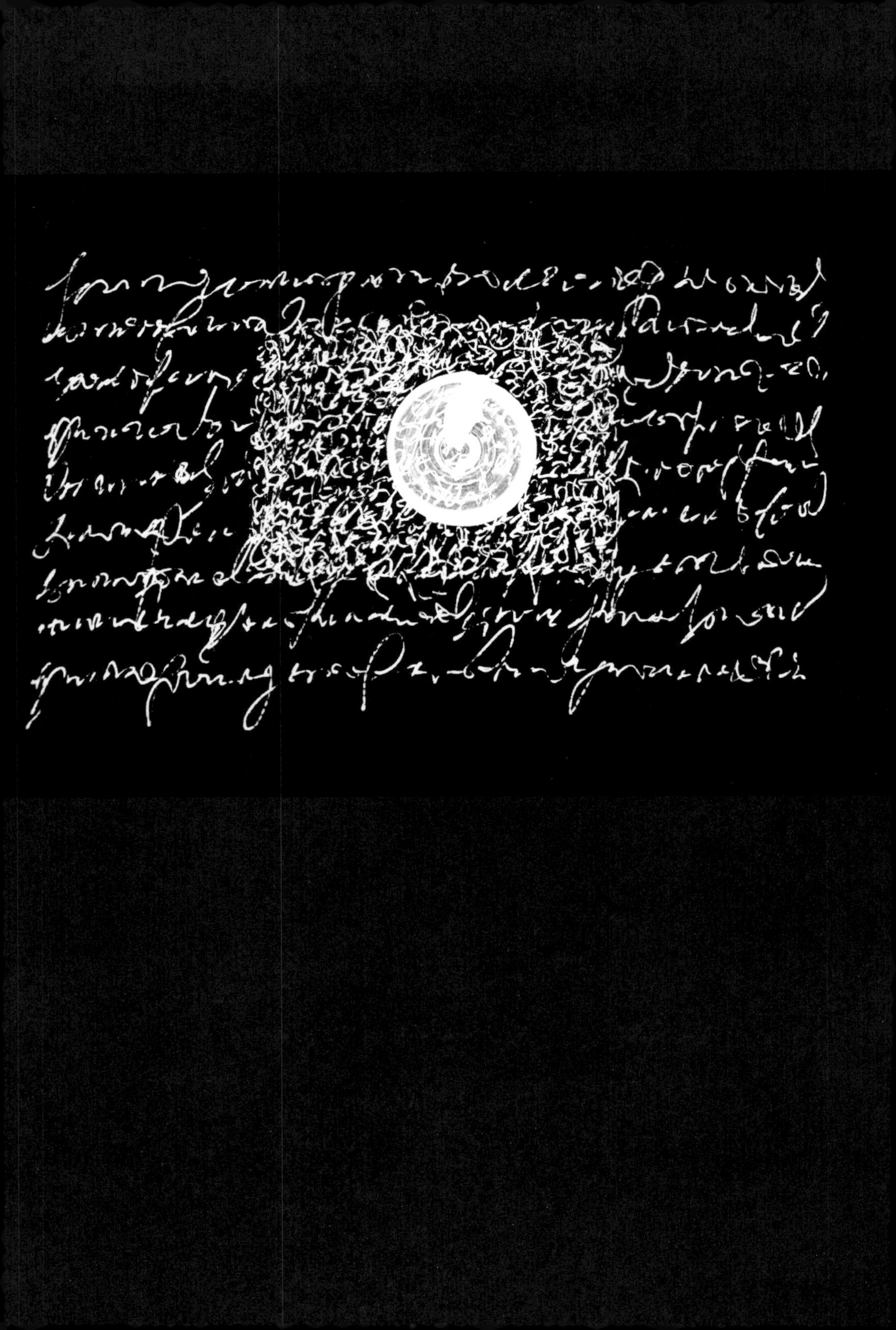

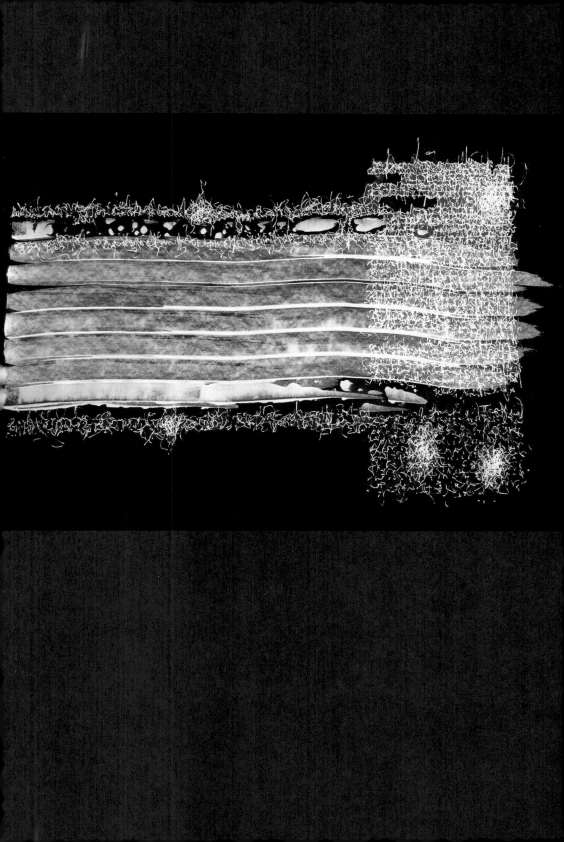

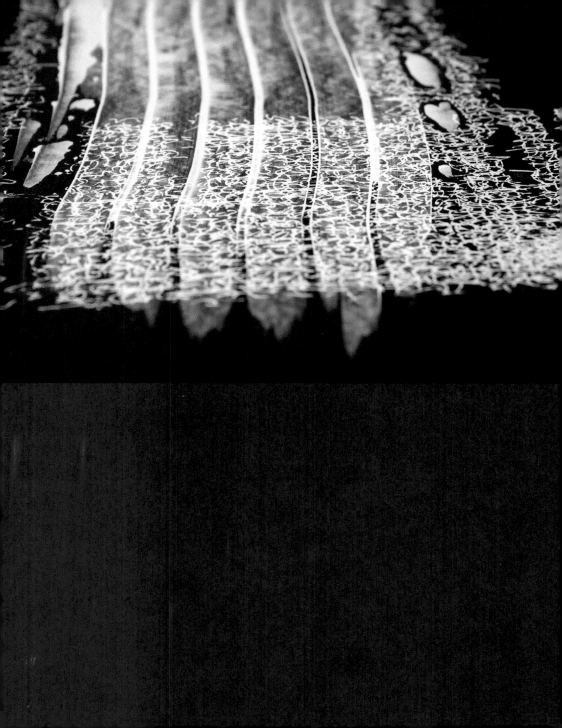

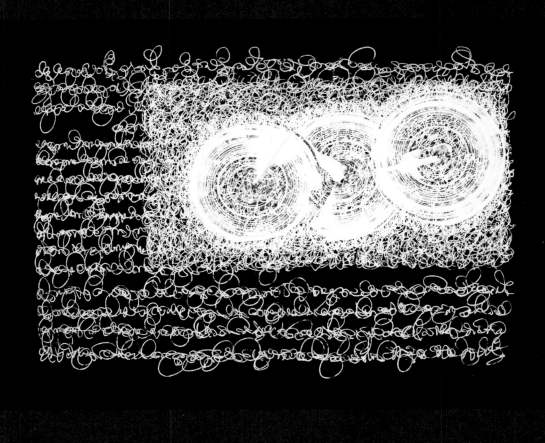

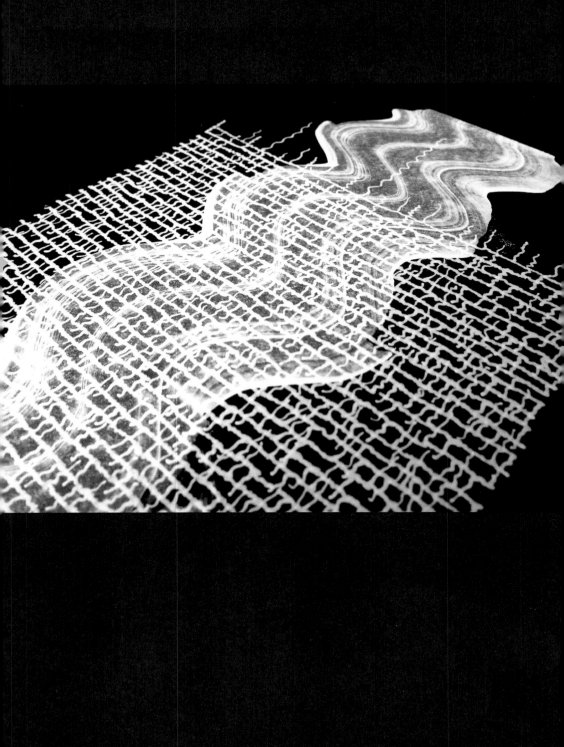

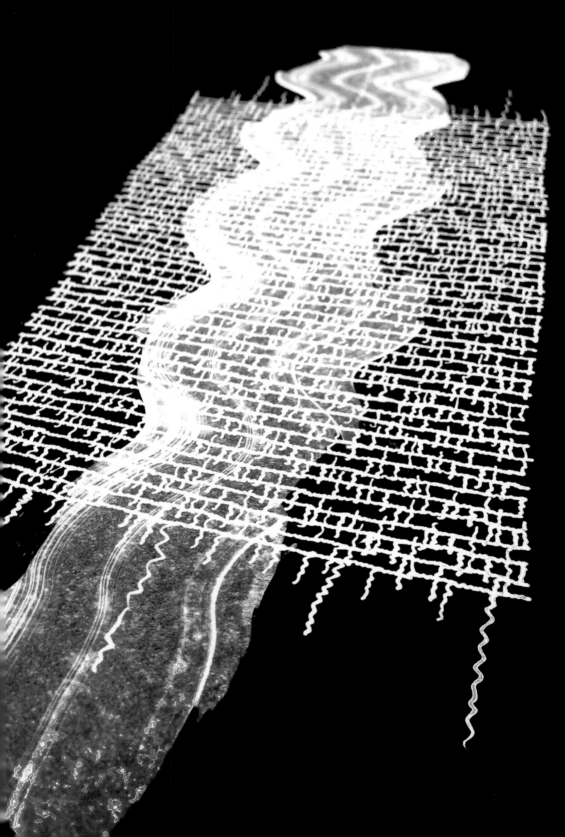

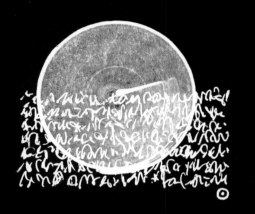

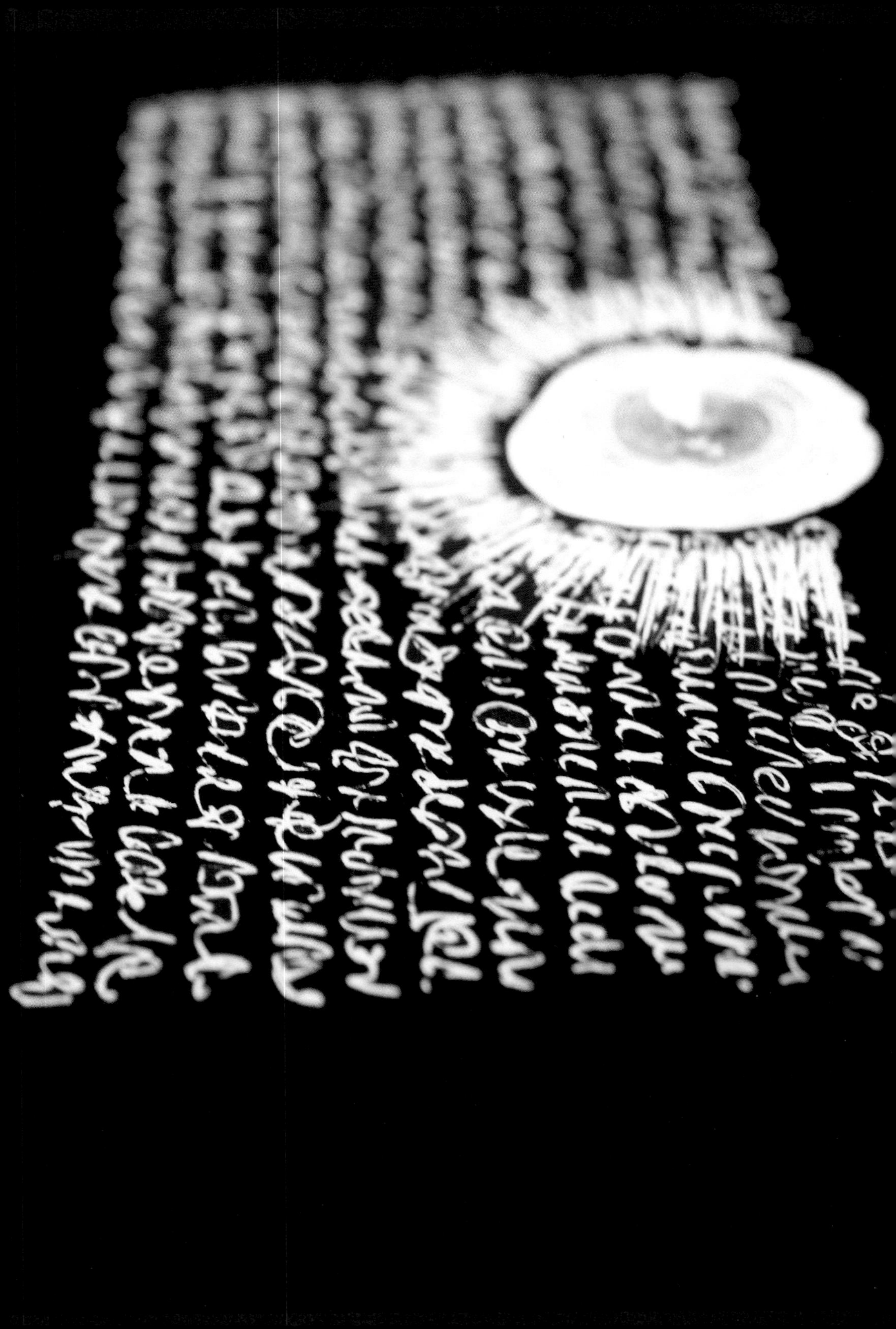

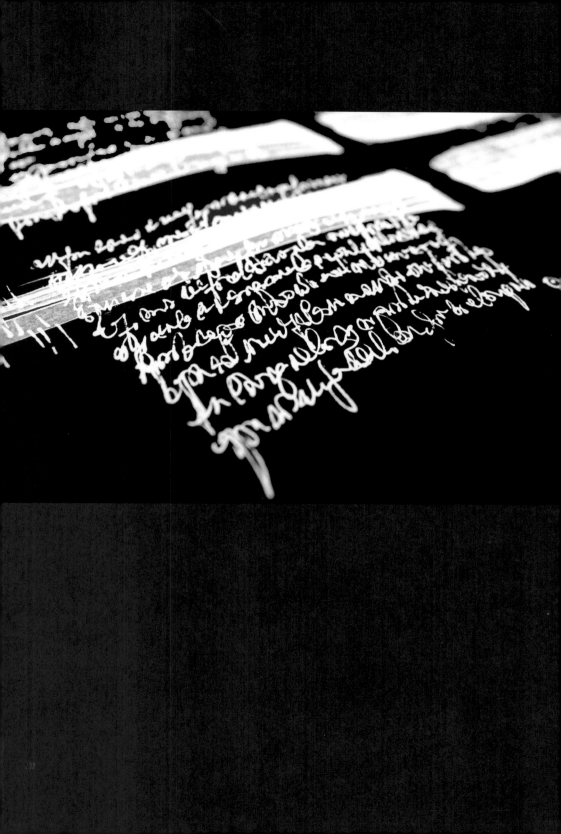

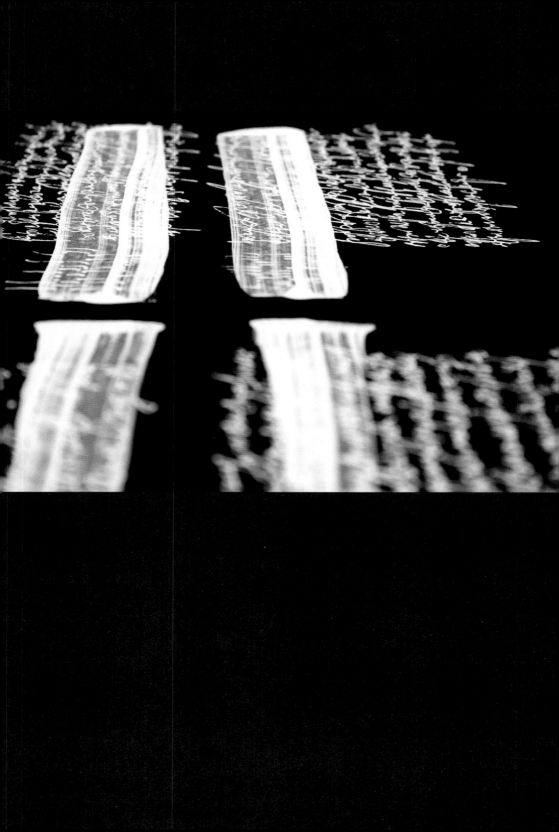

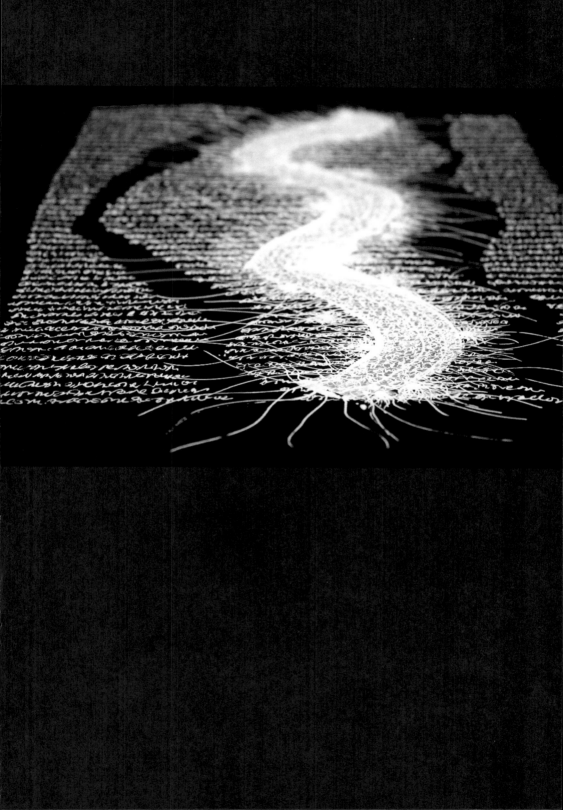

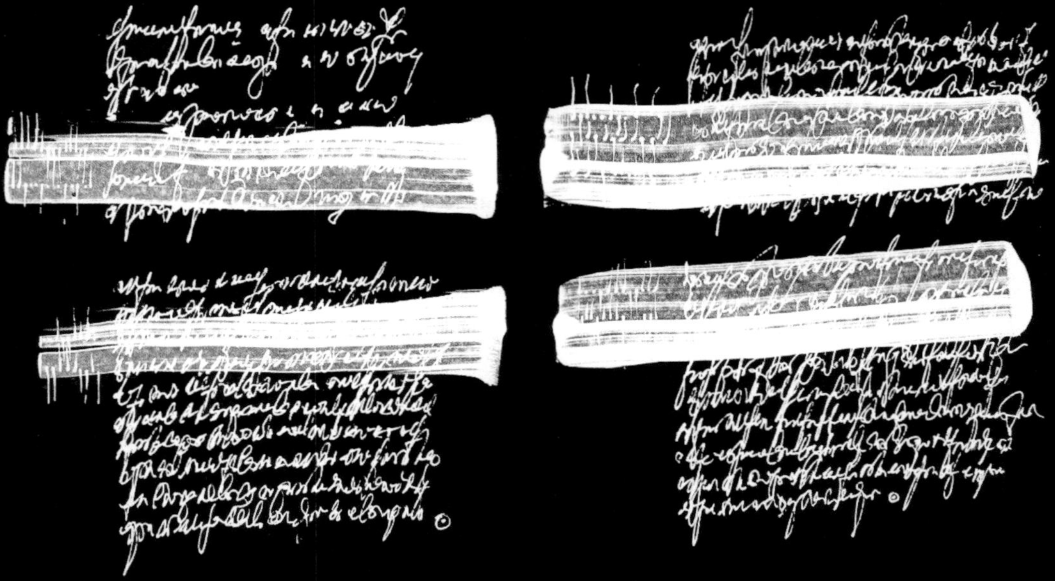

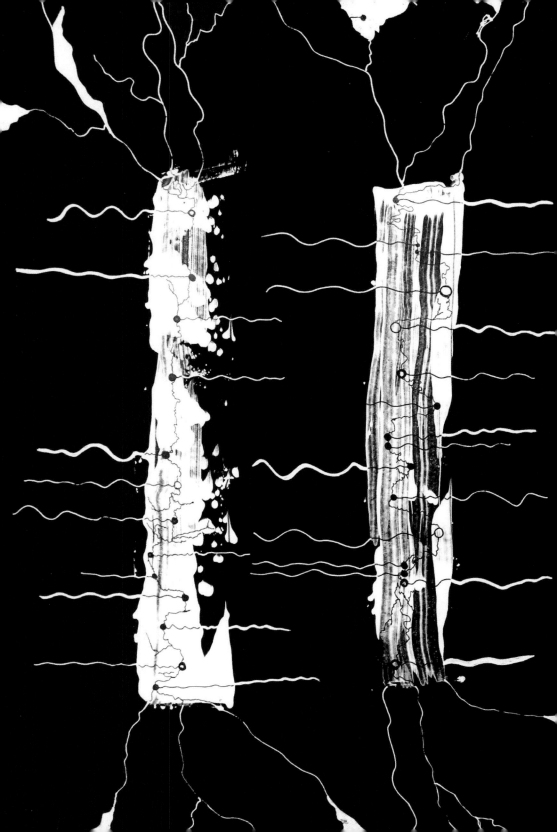

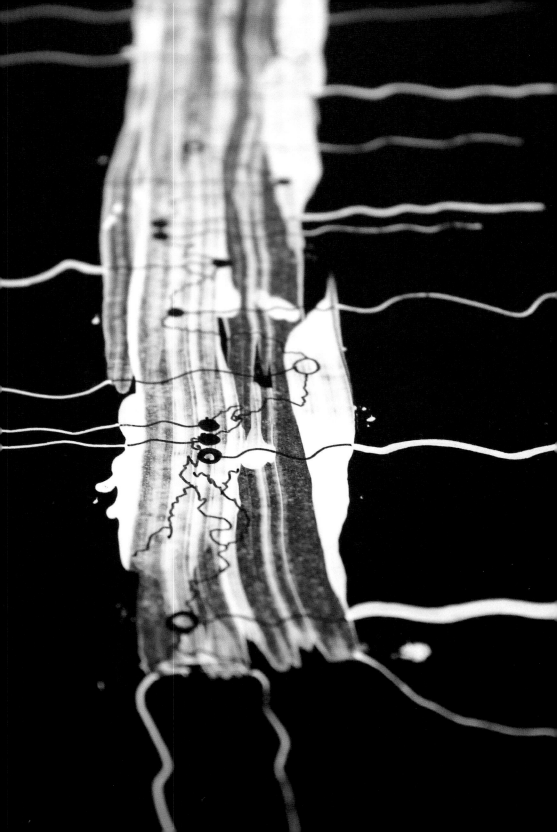

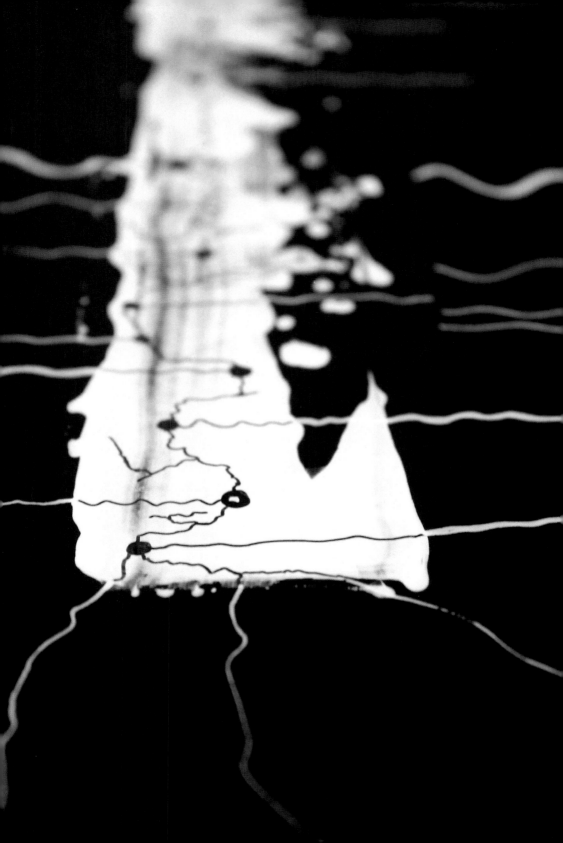

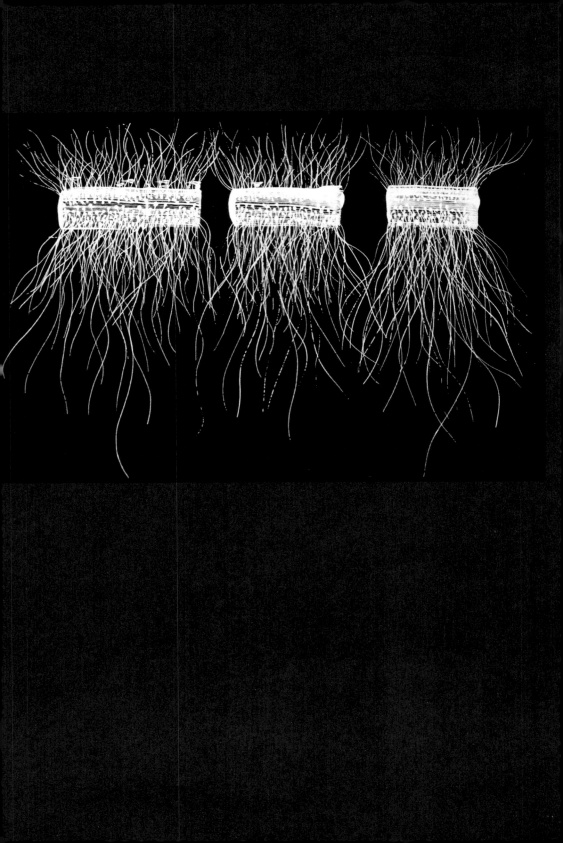

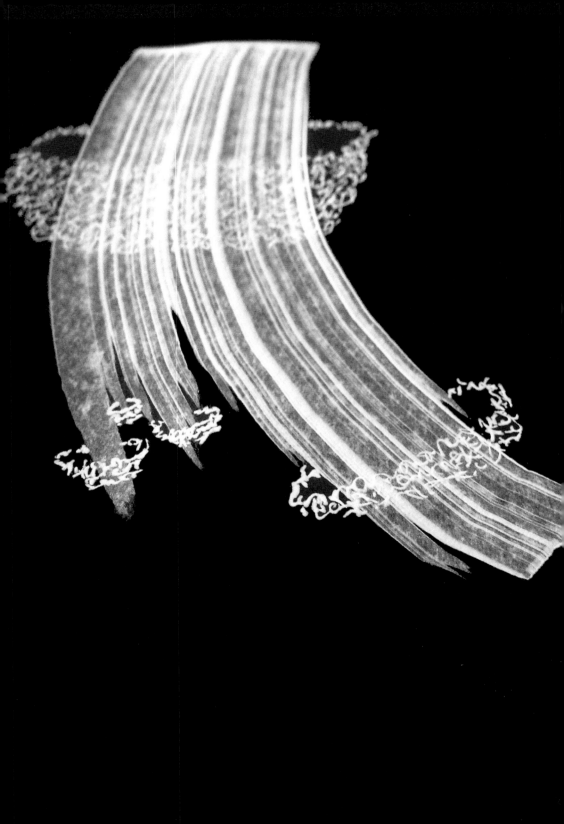

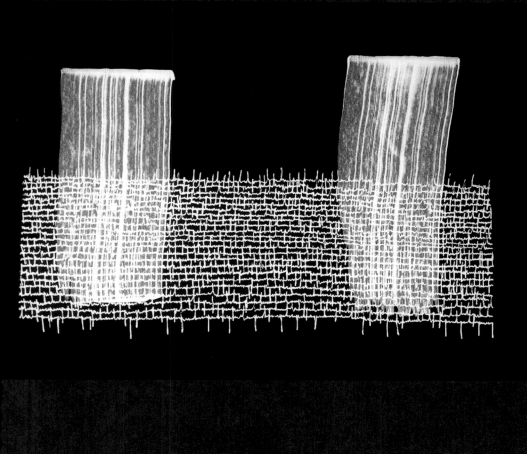

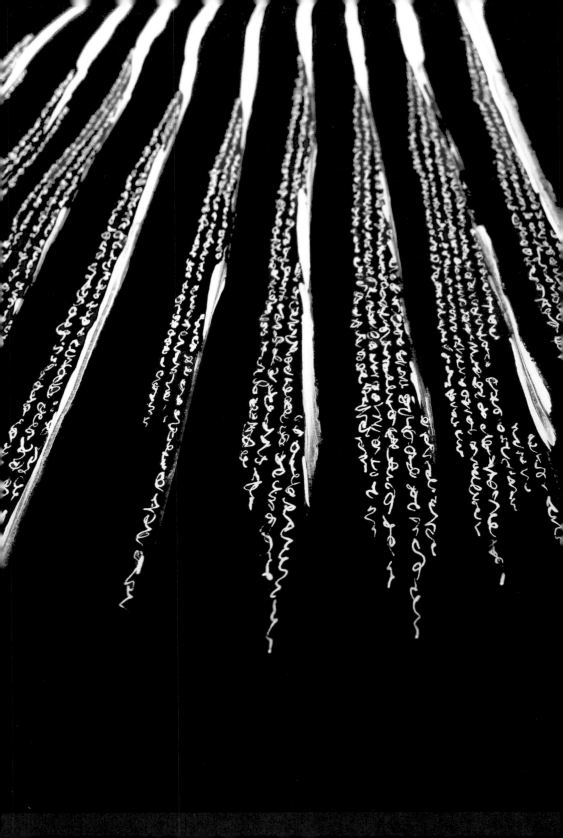

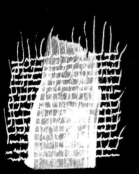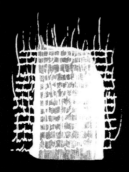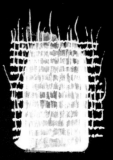
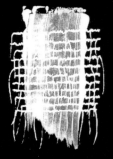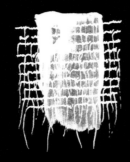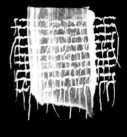

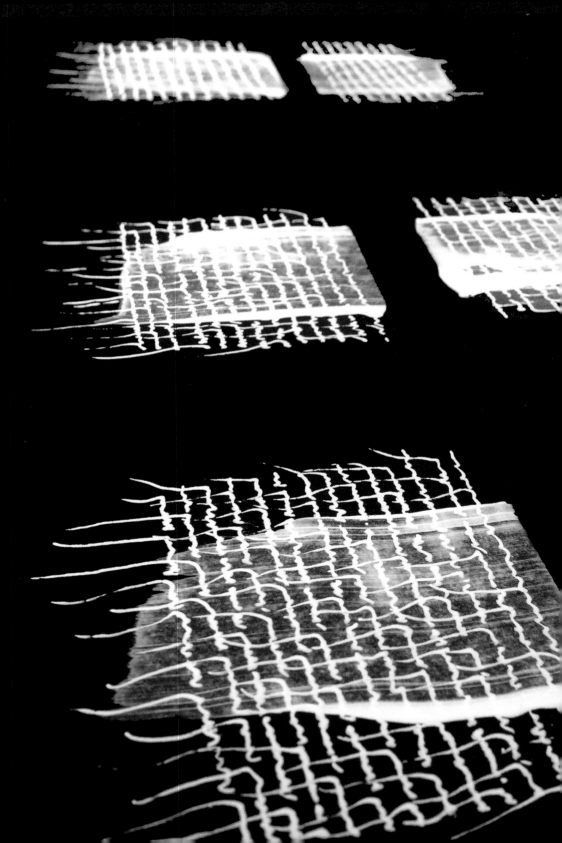

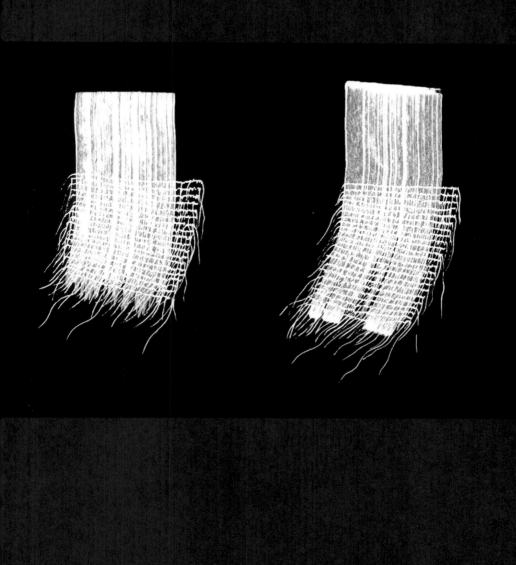

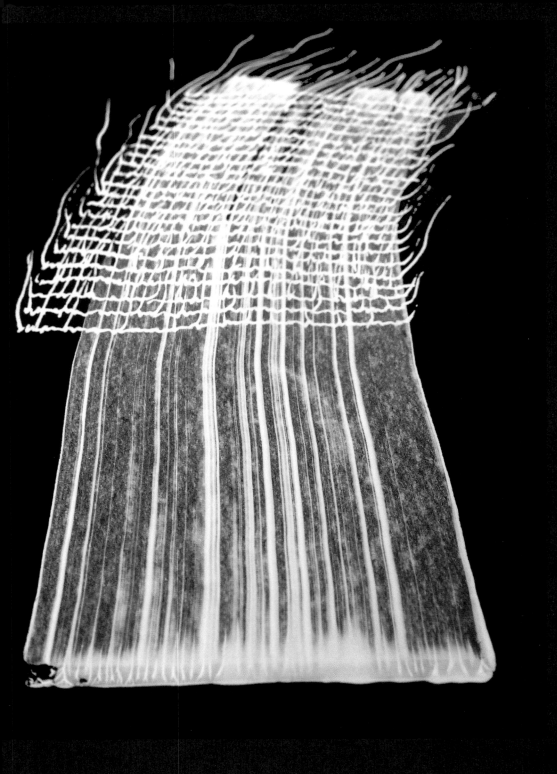

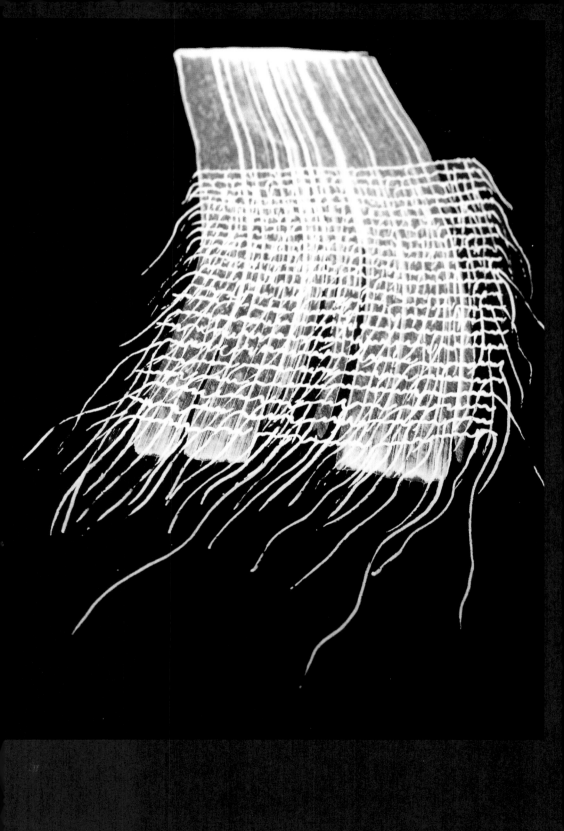

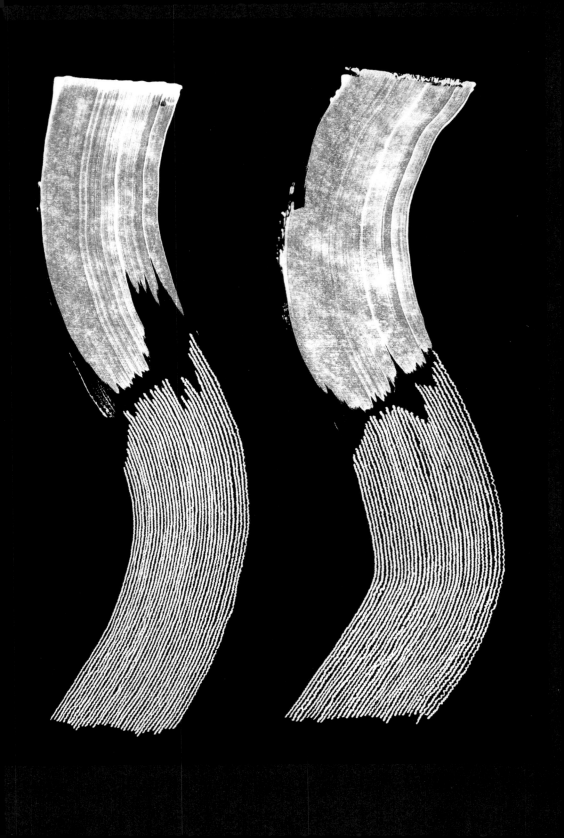

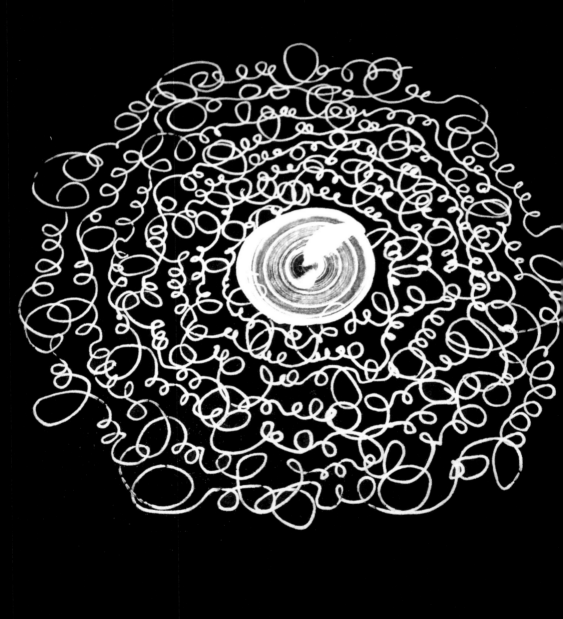

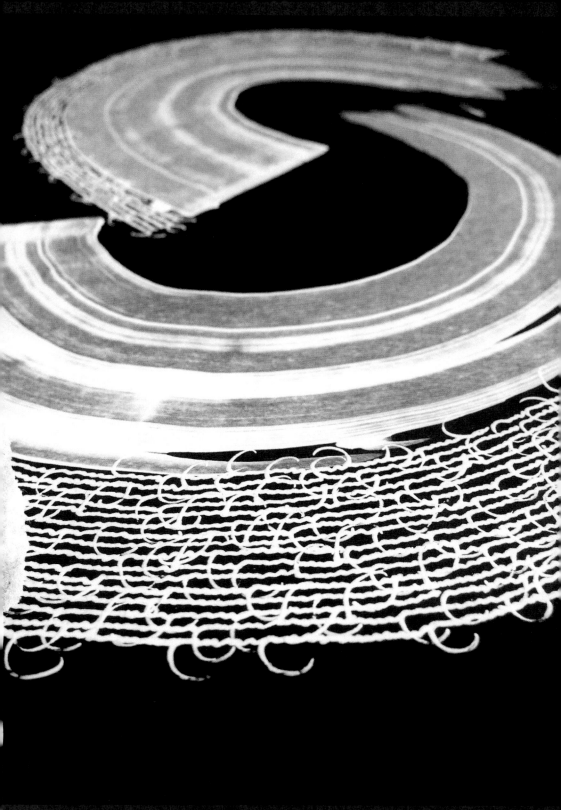

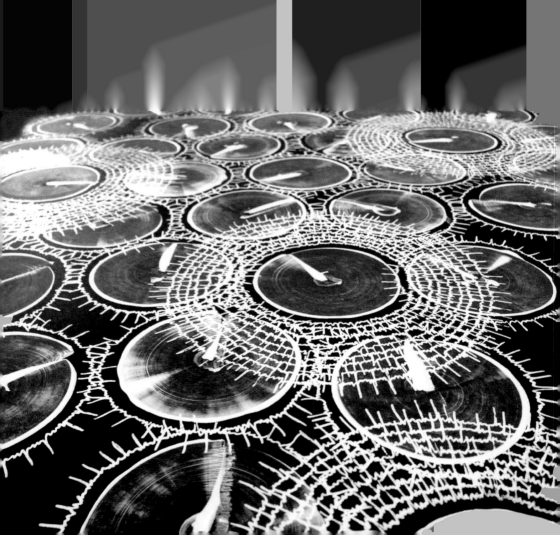

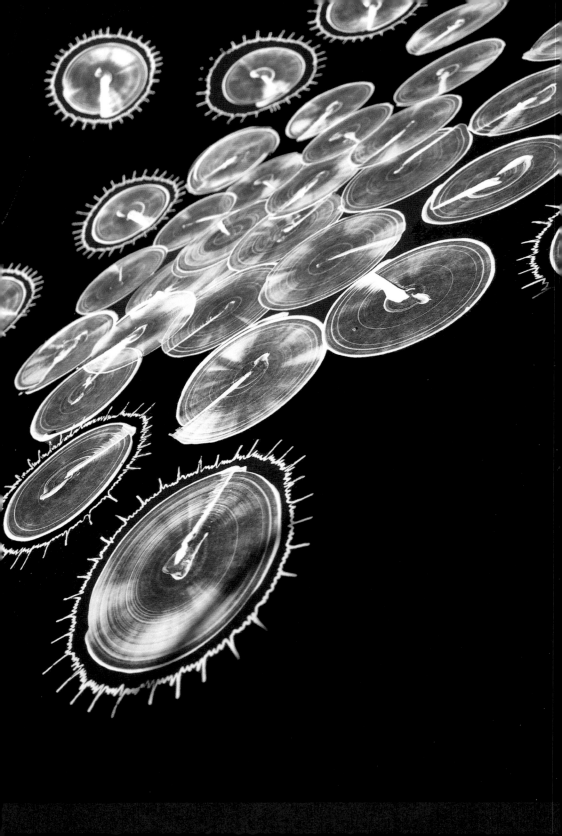

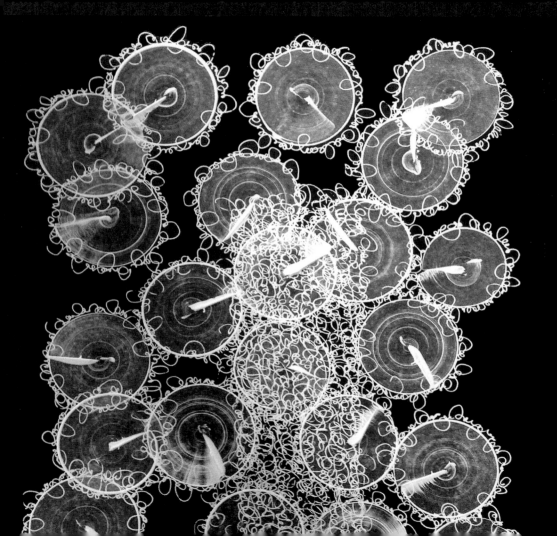

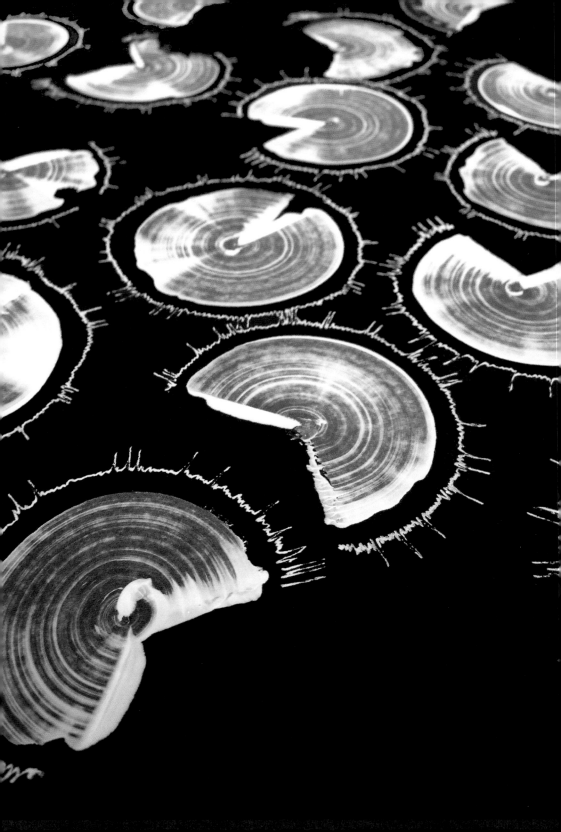

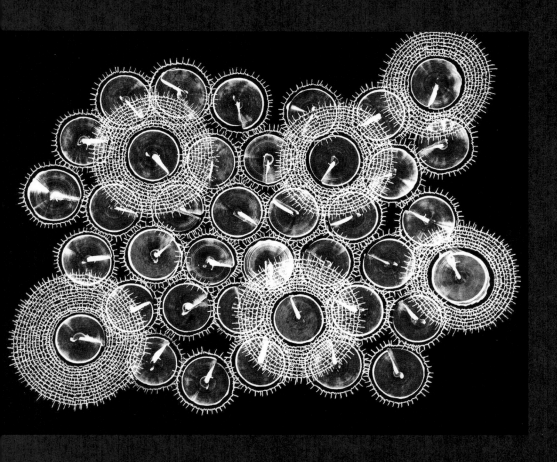

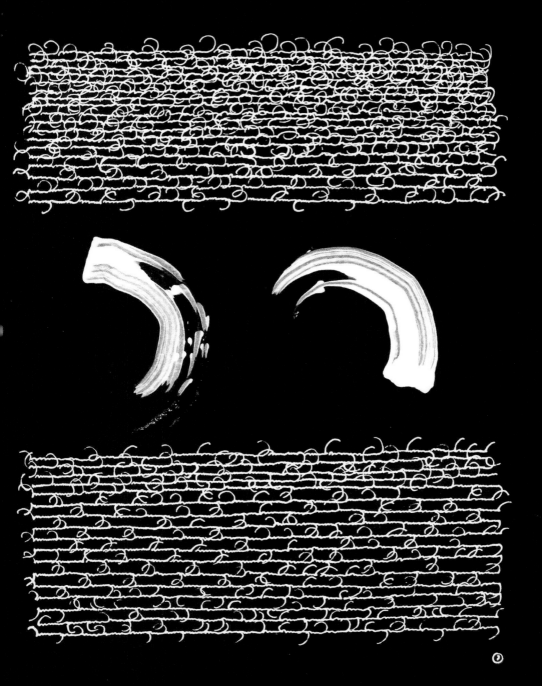

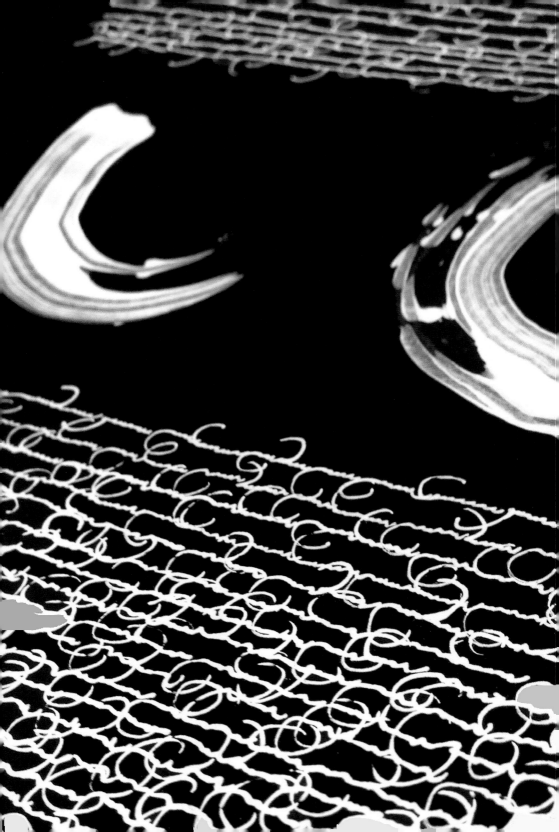

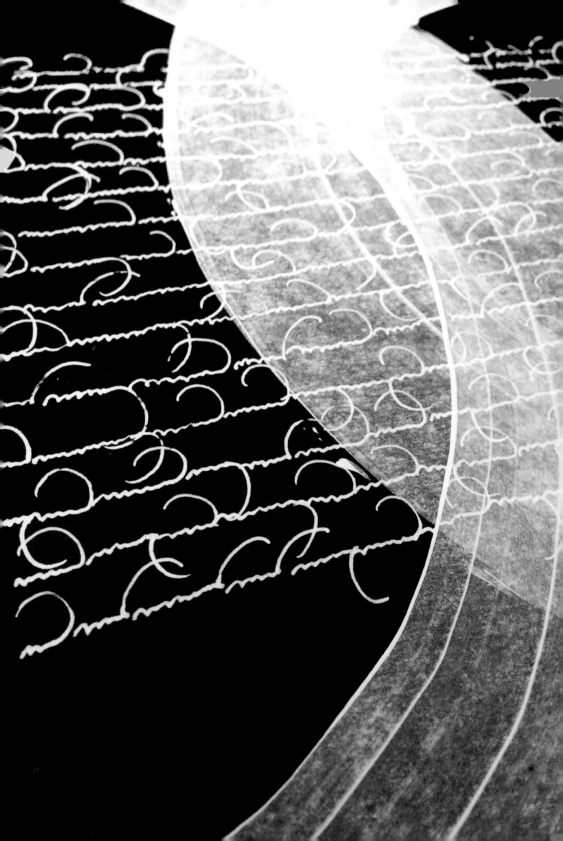

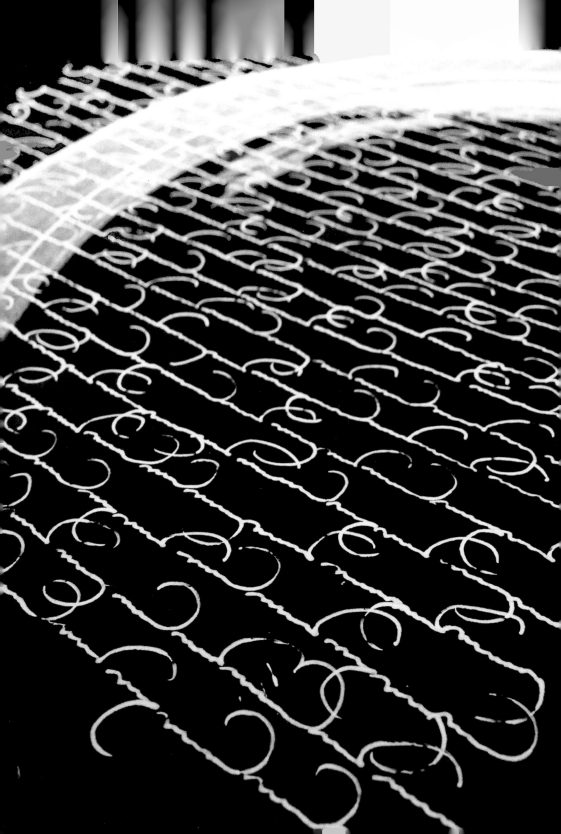

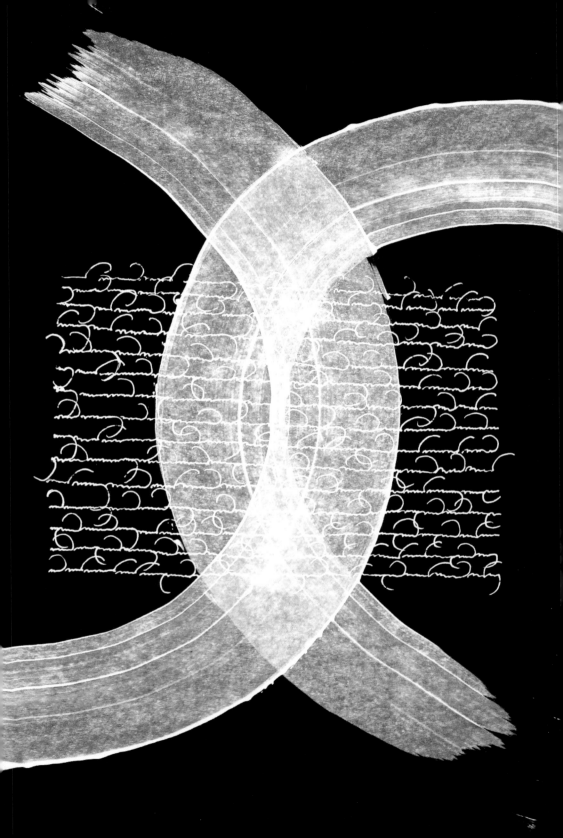

Born in Belgium, Anneke received an Education in the Arts, languages and Music. After much travel, she now resides in Sydney, Australia. Primarily an artist, secondly a rock climber she supplements these passions with a career in publishing and marketing. Multi-disciplined, her focus is on asemic writing and expressing concepts in visual poetry. When quizzed about her creative process Anneke compared asemic expression being akin to letting out the bunch of crazy ferrets running around in her head. That analogy has stuck and is now the collective name behind Anneke's artistic presence. She looks to constantly push the boundaries of her ability and style with the ink barely dry on the last piece before a new goal appears and her fingers start to itch for a new canvas. Her art has been published online in Otoliths,Truck, Utsanga, The New Post-Literate, Coldfront Extreme writing Community Blog, and Sonic Boom. She has been featured in a number of anthology publications (ALPHA BET A TEST: The Eye Am Eye Asemic Anthology: Language in the Act of Disappearing Edited by Paul A. Toth, 2015), RENEGADE (Andrew Topel, publishing late 2017) and has exhibited in many international group exhibitions and has enjoyed a solo exhibition at Curve Gallery

CPSIA information can be obtained at www.ICGtesting.com
Printed in the USA
LVIW010136030620
657276LV00004B/6

* 9 7 8 1 7 3 2 8 7 8 8 4 6 *